LEADING
EXECUTIVE
CONVERSATIONS

WHAT BUSINESS EXECUTIVES HAVE TO SAY ABOUT SALLY WILLIAMSON AND *LEADING EXECUTIVE CONVERSATIONS*

"Leading Executive Conversations is a must read for managers looking to make a profound impact in the workforce. Sally's research and framework for effectively leading executive conversations allows managers to be prepared, succinct and captures the executive's attention, quickly allowing these conversations to be positive, career-defining moments."

Rebecca Dickey
Senior Manager
Accenture

"Leading Executive Conversations successfully brings Sally Williamson's world class expertise to life. It is clearly a must read for the leaders of today and tomorrow."

Jack Bergstrand
CEO
Brand Velocity, Inc.

"In my work I have opportunities to refer senior leaders to Sally to help them improve their executive presence. Sally and her team's process combined with their experience have proven to get results with clients. She understands what it is like to be an executive and how to develop and deliver impactful messages that engage and inspire followers."

David Brookmire
President
Corporate Performance Strategies

"Sally's books are filled with down-to-earth real problems and practical solutions. They are easy to read and easy to learn from. They cover the topics that are not the clichés of leadership, but the things you really need to know to become successful. For executives that care about their upcoming leaders and care enough to help those folks become better, you're always safe to recommend a read from Sally. And, it's a worthwhile read for you too."

Henrietta King
Vice President, Administrative and Strategic Services
The Southeast Permanente Medical Group, Inc.

"Sally truly transformed one of the leaders I asked her to coach; she is for real."

Sasan Goodarzi
Senior Vice President & General Manager
Consumer Tax Group
Intuit, Inc.

"My role as an innovation leader requires me to communicate with a wide variety of senior leaders both inside and outside the company. Sally's approach and techniques have extended my communication style so that I can confidently navigate critical executive conversations about change and innovation."

Mark Pearson
Senior Vice President, Manager of Innovation Programs
SunTrust Banks, Inc.

"Sally consistently demonstrates a gift for working with leaders and their teams, to help them function more effectively in all of their internal and external facing roles. She has a unique ability to assess the human and organizational dynamics of a leadership team and then quickly and concisely communicate ways to improve those dynamics."

Joanie Teofilo
President & CEO
The Energy Authority

"Sally has a unique talent for coaching leaders at all levels to communicate with confidence and executive presence. She understands the importance of presenting content through storytelling that simplifies and clarifies complex messages. She has helped me and many others on my team prepare for and deliver effective and high-impact communications for all types of audiences. I am truly grateful for her expertise."

Veronica Sheehan
Senior Vice President, Global Network, Technology and Studio Operations
Turner Broadcasting System, Inc.

"Sally and her team have been helping me with my executive communication strategies for years. They help facilitate superior executive communication and they instill confidence with their approach and expertise."

Paul T. Johnson
Executive Vice President, Sales and Services
Vocera Communications

LEADING EXECUTIVE CONVERSATIONS

BE CONFIDENT. BE COMPELLING. BE CONCISE.

SALLY WILLIAMSON

Published by Sally Williamson and Associates, Inc.
Two Buckhead Plaza
3050 Peachtree Road NW, Suite 520
Atlanta, GA 30305

ISBN 978-0-9837069-4-6
Library of Congress Control Number: 2014911681

DEDICATION

To Gwen, Hurst, and Katie

Approach your work with a passion so that your
passion may become your life's work.

Table of Contents

Section 1: The Situation

Section 2: The Solution

Section 3: The Impact

Section 4: The Rest of the Story

Section 5: The Complexities

Survey Results

What Managers Are Saying About Our Workshop

Template: Executive Conversation

Example: Executive Conversation Scenario

Example: Executive Conversation

Example: Executive Overview (Pre-Read)

Example: Executive Overview (Visual)

SW&A Content Planner

Acknowledgements

While putting words on a page is a solo assignment, this project expands well beyond these pages.

It has truly been a team effort at SW&A, and I am grateful for the dedication and passion embodied in the SW&A team. Thank you for the added support on this endeavor and the fun we always manage to have along the way.

I also owe many thanks to the executives who shared their time, insights, and perspectives to give me a starting point.

But most of all, my gratitude to the managers who opened up about their challenges and admitted a few failures. It was your stories that inspired the writing, and it is your determination to improve that will make you great leaders. I can't wait to see you succeed!

Section 1:

The Situation

1

The Manager's Perspective

"I want you to know that I've covered all the bases."

It's true what they say: be careful what you ask for.

Across every company and every career, a top priority of most managers is to gain visibility with the key leaders of the company. It's so coveted a destination that it takes on its own identity: The C-suite, the 20th floor, the leaders' level. The reason that most managers want to gain visibility is that they believe it leads to recognition, opportunities, and ultimately, promotions.

Early in your career, a promotion may be based on the perspective of one person: your immediate boss. But, as your role and responsibilities expand, so do the decisions surrounding your career path. The senior manager role or the VP position carries more weight and responsibility. A seasoned position has impact on the business results of a company. And, as a result, it will be vetted more thoroughly.

Without question, executive impressions are set in these conversations and meetings with middle managers. In fact, not only

3

are their impressions set, but executives also say that their impressions last until they interact with you again in a similar setting. So, that may mean one month or six months later, depending on the size of your company.

While the opportunity to gain visibility is what most managers crave, the old adage comes to mind again: be careful what you ask for.

Visibility isn't that hard to get, and some will tell you they got it a little sooner than they expected. The question is: Will you be ready for the opportunity, and will you have the skills to lead this conversation?

These meetings aren't easy according to most managers. In fact, 90% of them say it's a harder meeting; 20% of those say it's significantly more difficult than other meetings.

Most will tell you that the chance to lead an executive conversation comes with a fair amount of notice. You'll be invited because you have the results of a large initiative or insights into a new market segment. You may be the subject matter expert or the leader of a project, or you can gain access to the top floor via another leader or even from your own initiative.

Once that date is confirmed, you'll begin pulling reams of information and data points together to back up your conclusions. You're smart enough to know that this is the communication situation you should sweat, and you will.

You'll feel more prepared for this conversation than most others you have within the company. You are excited about this opportunity and recognize it as a chance to show your level of knowledge and expertise on the topic.

With the best of intentions, you'll still make all of the wrong choices, because the executive doesn't want to know what you know; he or she wants to know what the company should do based on your knowledge.

- You'll present a lot of data; the executive wants context.
- You'll dive deep into the implementation of a plan; they want to know why the plan is needed.
- You'll share your perspective; they're interested in everyone else's.
- You'll design a forty-slide PowerPoint deck; they prefer a one-page summary.

These are all examples of the earnest manager meeting the impatient executive.

In our research, managers told us that these high-level conversations go poorly almost 40% of the time. That's a dangerous statistic for a career-defining moment. In my thirty years as a coach, over and over again, I have seen the disconnect that exists between what managers do and what executives want. In most cases, it comes down to a difference in perspectives: managers say that the best approach to a thirty-minute meeting is to plan out twenty minutes pretty tightly.

"Present your ideas and your recommendation in twenty minutes. Be well-rehearsed and try to give as many points to validate your ideas as you can in that twenty minutes. Save five minutes for questions. Ideally, the executive will let you lead the conversation and take questions at the end. Practice repeatedly to be sure that you have your timing down well and that the 'conversation' is over in under thirty minutes."

This manager's best intentions are driven by his own perspective and agenda for this conversation. That's where the mistake begins. In order to lead high-level conversations, you need to know what executives value and how they plan to participate in the conversation.

2

The Executive's Perspective

*"It's true that when you are in leadership,
your attention span shortens."*

While executives agree they can be impatient, unfocused, and sometimes disruptive, they are extremely consistent in what they look for in conversations.

Well over 90% of the executives we interviewed said, "I want to know what you need from me and why you believe this action can impact our business. Eliminate the details and stay focused on what you are trying to accomplish with me."

They expect to participate. In fact, when asked what they thought would be the best approach to a thirty-minute meeting, most said they expect to interact with the manager within five minutes. So, that buttoned-up plan to talk *at* them for twenty minutes isn't going to work so well.

Executives believe that they have value to add, and they are right. They have a very different view of the company, and they can expand topics or narrow discussion to link your initiative to other initiatives within the company. One executive told me,

> "The reason managers should meet with me is to connect the dots. I know things they don't know, and I have the broader perspective to decide if their initiatives are in alignment with the total picture."

They are very clear about the role they should play. High-level meetings exist to establish buy-in and to drive decisions. Executives move from one scenario to the next with a focused approach to taking action or moving a topic forward. The more disciplined executive demands that the topic and outcome are defined in pre-reads before the meeting takes place. Some even demand ten-minute meetings!

While seasoned managers lead these discussions four times a year, or even up to once a month, the executives themselves are in these conversations much more frequently. Most executives meet with a manager at least twice a week, and many have three to four of these meetings every day.

Just imagine how quickly they reach information overload with the number of meetings and data points they receive! Good leaders aren't sponges, and their role isn't simply to absorb information. They synthesize information and make choices to pull and push on different levers within a company to drive business results.

They are straight forward about what they want from these conversations, and most admit to being somewhat disruptive in order to get it. When asked if they interrupt in meetings, close to 95% said yes, but they are quick to say that they interrupt to "help out."

> "I don't want to be tough, but I need to get us through it. I need to be productive with the thirty minutes."

> "I offer a helping hand. I'll ask questions to try and help you get on track. But if you can't, I'm quick to say I have a hard stop. Then, I'll give your manager more direct feedback, and you aren't likely to be in another meeting with me for a while."

> "I don't redirect because I know it throws the manager off. I'm a little worse. I let managers get themselves out on a limb, and when time runs out I say we need to reschedule to get through this, but I rarely take the next meeting."

Focused executives know that these conversations should yield direction and decisions that help move topics forward, yet they say that close to 30% of the meetings they attend are run poorly. So, they jump in to redirect the conversation and drive the discussion to an outcome and decision. Sometimes, they get a little frustrated in the process.

> "Don't invite me to a status update on all the wonderful work you are doing; I don't have time for show-and-tell."

> "Don't bring me a problem without a few potential solutions."

> "The only perspective you had on this topic was your own. Why would a leader change a business strategy based on one perspective?"

"Don't tell me that you know a lot; show me why it matters."

"I can expand your thinking and help you find a simpler way to solve."

"I can connect things that may not otherwise be connected. I want to help you."

While they were all managers once themselves, they've forgotten the limited focus that managers often have, and they rarely see the need to know "everything" you know about a topic.

They have little patience for conversations that don't move toward an outcome, and their impression of managers who can't drive conversations forward is generally negative. One leader told me that he gave it three tries. The manager showed up poorly in front of him three times, and then he asked the manager's EVP not to bring him back again. Other executives talked about the point of no return in the same way. A few misses, and they aren't likely to want you in meetings. Some say it's because they don't value your input; others because they worry that it really is damaging your brand.

This is a high-risk communication situation. There is a great upside to leading these conversations well. Without question, it can be a career advancement step, but there are significant consequences as well. In each interview, we asked executives to share examples of poorly-run meetings, and the examples are plentiful.

There is no doubt that a senior-level conversation can be tough, but my experience is that they can also be predictable. And, that's the goal of this book. Based on over thirty years' experience in executive coaching and workshops, I believe that a better understanding of the executive perspective and a clear framework that meets their expectations can yield great outcomes. Over the next eighteen chapters, I'm going to provide insight into what executives want, why they want it, and a framework that can help you organize your ideas into a storyline that executives value.

You aren't likely to see the C-suite soften up or attend meetings without expectations. So, this may always be the communication situation that managers should sweat, but you can improve your game by focusing on what they need to understand your topic and aligning your topic with the business outcomes they drive every day.

3

The Dilemma

"I went into the meeting prepared to run the bases, and I ended up in left field without a glove."

I t's fair to say that the disconnect that exists in high-level meetings doesn't rest solely on the shoulders of the manager. Executives admit that they are part of the challenge, but more effective results come from understanding the executives' perspectives and giving them information they value, rather than hoping they'll adjust their expectations.

So, what goes wrong?

Executives say it's a lack of preparation and focus. Our survey results identified these top four issues from the executives' perspectives:

- I ask things they are unprepared to answer.
- They present too much detail. It's not high-level enough.
- The presenter can't make his/her point effectively.
- There is no clear takeaway.

You can see that the executive feels the meeting needs more focus and less detail. While they want you to be prepared to answer anything, they actually don't want you to cover everything in the discussion. That can be a little confusing to the manager who has been coached to be well-prepared. Through our interviews, I've learned that being well-prepared means being ready to answer questions and provide a certain level of detail when asked for it, but managers interpret preparation as presenting just the details. They are taking in too much material to cover, and the result is information overload. Executives are just too impatient to wait for you to build an idea from the bottom up.

> "I have a mid-level manager who is unable to communicate succinctly. Meetings trail all over the universe, and I have to pull her out of the weeds to get to the point. I find it difficult to focus on the issues she raises, and I can be dismissive of her expertise – all because I didn't understand where the conversation was headed."

> "Without a clear starting point, I often feel that managers have no idea of what they're asking for and no clear vision of why they want it."

> "Managers just seem to struggle with getting their points across."

These comments shed light on the executives' needs for a clear takeaway and a clear ask in the meeting. In Chapter 5, I'll show you how to create a compelling message and takeaway. It's the number one thing they listen for, as you can see from the next statements.

"Managers struggle to roll-up their ideas to a business strategy. So, it's up to me to link your idea to the strategy. It should be the other way around."

"I don't need loads of background; I need a theme that is compelling."

"A manager came into the meeting with no recommendation and no sense of the impact of the problem. He just brought us the problem."

"When you don't have a mastery of the facts or the ask, you just seem unprepared."

The truth is that it's easier to go into meetings loaded with information. It's much harder to sift through the information to get to relevant points and clear takeaways, and the executives' demands for that clarity are what makes them the tougher audience. In their own words, executives sound like a more focused and more challenging audience.

In fact, when managers are asked what goes wrong in meetings, they say the executives cause most of the problems. Our survey results identified these top four issues from the managers' perspectives:

- I was rushed.
- The executive side tracked the meeting.
- I didn't get through all my material as planned.
- The meeting was cut short.

These comments suggest they started from a more buttoned-up approach. While the manager may feel prepared, he is going into the meeting too rehearsed and too overloaded with information to drive a more high-level conversation.

Most managers admit this causes problems. When they shared examples of their worst meetings, the themes were consistent with the survey results.

"I just wasn't prepared with the exact thing I needed."

"I was prepared to discuss the topic, but not his questions surrounding the topic."

"I was unclear about what was being asked for and what was needed."

"I started the meeting without a clear and stated objective, and it was off track in a matter of minutes."

"I was asked to provide details on a bad situation. I spent a lot of time preparing my thoughts and materials to support what had happened. Within minutes, the executive told me that we should be focused on discussing what we could do to prevent recurrence, rather than how we got into the situation. I was totally unprepared for that discussion."

"I was caught off guard by the questions asked and felt unprepared for the discussion. This made me nervous and unsure of my responses, and I know it showed. So, I requested that we schedule a second meeting so I could come back with the type of information the executive wanted. I never got the second meeting."

"I was so excited by my first executive-level meeting that I over-prepared. I went in with a three-page agenda and thought I would be able to cover all of it. I got through the first three bullet points and realized the meeting was halfway over. I rushed through the material and learned my lesson about going in with information versus a point of view and direction."

We've all been there, and we know that the pressure and the circumstances can make it worse. Some managers say the executives don't pay attention; one even said the executive fell asleep! Many managers go to meetings that are cut short or are interrupted by phones, emails, or other executives. In fact, executives themselves recognize the dilemma.

"The challenge for managers is to articulate an objective and a strategy and to know the difference."

"I know they feel pressure to perform, and they should. There just aren't a lot of chances to do well."

"Managers feel that as long as they're talking, we're making progress. That's just not the case. Don't confuse activity with progress."

"Most managers are so focused on telling me every bit of information they know that it makes them appear scattered. Ugh!"

"It's all about focus. Meetings just seem to lack it. In every meeting, I challenge managers to think about what we're doing and why. When the manager can do that, I sit up and take notice."

"Managers don't take time to understand my knowledge level, so we're quickly operating on two different levels."

"I should be the editor. If I have to be the author and the editor, why are we meeting?"

One of the most common disconnects with executives can be seen in IT conversations. There are two different levels of understanding in the room, and IT managers often want to establish a deep level of understanding with their leadership. At the root of it is the desire to be valued for what they're trying to accomplish.

Most IT presentations I see start with a level of detail designed to drive towards that understanding. The conversation is heavy in how things work and step-by-step explanations of process. Executives get frustrated wading through the technological details. They say, "I don't ask them to understand my business; I don't think I should have to understand the details of theirs." IT managers get frustrated by the lack of interest, and executives get lost in the details and process. It goes without saying that we've restructured a lot of high-level conversations for IT managers.

However, IT managers are not alone in their struggles with executive conversations. Managers and executives of various backgrounds and fields were interviewed, and they were all in agreement.

Managers say these high-level conversations are more difficult, and executives agree they are definitely different conversations. In fact, one executive recalled his first meeting when he walked into the CEO's office and made the mistake of thinking he was just there for a chat. Executives are quick to point out that their time shouldn't be used for brainstorming or vetting ideas.

"You can't treat this conversation like a chat with a coworker."

"Don't confuse interactive with informal."

"I don't want you to think out loud with me; you should think it through and then bring me the core context."

"Executive discussion is about decision-making. Managers talk to each other for ideas and brainstorming."

The executive quotes and stories are full of frustration with meetings that don't drive results, and unfortunately, they take action on their impressions. Here are a few stories that illustrate how strong those impressions can be:

"One manager came to me pretty set in her ways about why we couldn't implement an on-boarding program on the timetable that I wanted. Rather than giving me options and thinking creatively about how we could accomplish it, she dug in her heels and set up roadblocks about why it wouldn't work. From my vantage point, we needed to bring on new hires in order to meet business demand, and we needed to find a way to accelerate the on-boarding process. Her inability to see the business need rather than her own agenda made a lasting impression on me. To this day, I limit interactions with her and do not consider her beyond her current role."

"A manager came to me to discuss an issue. He did not understand the history behind the issue, and he did not know the answer to any of my questions. It was as if he only knew what pertained to him and did not know why, how, or what the other pieces of the puzzle were. I knew he wasn't ready for high-level conversations, and I haven't invited him to a meeting in two years."

"A seasoned manager didn't adapt his approach in a meeting when he clearly needed to do so. I gave him two opportunities to redirect the focus, and he continued to stay the course with his planned comments. That was it; he hasn't been back."

"A manager came to a meeting unprepared and didn't have the information on-hand that I needed in order to make a final decision. I ended up asking a lot of questions to unearth the information I needed; I felt like an investigative reporter! I felt I was put in a position to push the manager rather than in a position to assist her. I left the meeting with little information, no next steps, and a bad impression of the manager."

One executive offered this advice for solving the dilemma of the gap between the two perspectives:

"People walk into meetings and don't have confidence in themselves. When that happens, no matter what the topic, it comes across as weak. If you've been working on a project for five months, you know way more than I do. Stand by that knowledge, but you have to get our conversation started on common ground."

A good understanding of what executive's value and what they listen for will help you get to that common ground. For a full summary of the survey results, see the Appendix at the end of the book.

4

Common Ground

---

*"I understand why you want to meet with me, but you
need to answer why I want to meet with you."*

Our surveys and interviews affirmed that executives
are tough in meetings, and they will be the first to
admit it. However, they are also predictable and consistent about what they expect to hear. The conversation won't
be easy because it takes preparation, but the concepts introduced
in this book are proven to align with the executive's perspective.

So, how do you get to common ground? Executives say they
expect the following:

- A topic that is relevant and timely.
- A clear understanding of what the manager needs from the
  executive.
- A clear recommendation or solution tied to the topic.
- A topic that aligns with a business need or priority.

Their quotes prove this:

> "You need to approach every conversation thinking that I have a role in the conversation."

> "Practice making a point and then stick to your point. If my first question throws you off, then my assumption is you weren't very committed to your point to start with."

> "Know how your topic aligns with the overall business strategy. If your recommendation has a 2% impact on the bottom-line and in the next meeting I attend the recommendation has a 20% impact, that's a pretty easy decision for me."

> "Start with the end in mind. If I'm clear about where we're headed, I'm more likely to stay on the course."

Overall, executives base their impressions on two things. First, "Is this person credible and confident?" In other words, "Should this person be talking to me?" Their response to your style happens in less than two minutes, and Chapter 11 will take you through the core ingredients of an executive presence and impressions. If you don't show up with confidence, the conversation isn't likely to last long.

But, confidence isn't enough for the executive audience. In addition, they want to see that you can solve a business need. In fact, they turn down the requests of confident people because they just don't see the priority or alignment with their business objectives.

In order to get to common ground, I believe you need to answer three key things:

What's your point? Executives listen for a message or takeaway at the start of every meeting. In Chapter 5, I'll show you how to create a message that drives an action or an ask from the executive and a measureable impact for the business.

How are we going to get there? Even when the takeaway is clear, you're dealing with an impatient listener, so the storyline of your conversation has to follow a framework that delivers context while keeping the discussion moving towards an impact. Both the message and the framework validate your ability to lead the conversation, and that's an essential element to avoid derailment by the executive. In Chapter 6, I'll introduce a framework that creates the context and momentum for this conversation.

Can you prove your ideas? Executives also look for proof points behind every idea. It isn't enough that it's your idea; they want validation throughout the discussion that gives them a reason to buy in to a recommendation or motivation to move forward with an initiative. In Chapter 8, we'll talk about proof points and how to make ideas memorable and repeatable.

If you can learn to answer those three questions, you'll find executive conversations can reach common ground. How do I know this? I know because I've used the concepts for over thirty years. As a small business owner, I've led many executive conversations to position our services and to predict the business impact we can make. I relate to the middle managers' perspectives and desires to deliver meaningful ideas, but more importantly,

I've coached to the executives' perspectives. I've heard their feedback and frustration for many years, and I began to recognize similarities among this audience. Across diverse industries and senior-level roles, I've seen consistency in expectations and core ingredients they need for decision-making.

Executives are predictable, and you can meet their expectations. When you do, both executives and managers agree that the outcomes of these conversations can have great benefits. All say that leading executive conversations gives you visibility in a company, and over 90% link success in these conversations to promotions. In one interview, an executive said,

> "While formal presentations get you noticed, it's your interaction with me in a smaller setting that makes you memorable."

Unfortunately, visibility comes with high stakes. Many managers we interviewed said they learned how to read the executive perspective the hard way, as their stories suggest.

> "I led a meeting for my boss with our top executive. The executive was clearly angry about this controversial topic and really wanted to vent and get to the bottom of why it happened. I tried to stick to my presentation and our points, and the more I pushed forward, the angrier he got. I missed the body language; I missed the point of the meeting. I've learned the hard way to frame up the situation."

> "I went in to give a project overview and didn't align my update with the whole scope of the project. Within five min-

utes, I was trying to backtrack and just couldn't get in sync with the executive."

"I've learned to tell them what you're asking for up front, but I learned it the hard way. I led a major initiative within our company and went into the senior leadership team's monthly meeting with updates. I found the team difficult to align and felt that my updates always went off track. I rarely got through my information. By the third month, I got feedback that the executives didn't think I was competent to run the project. My manager worked hard to help me hold onto the role, but I never presented the updates again."

"I was asked questions around data that I forgot to bring to the meeting. Instead of asking for a moment to go get it, I guessed at it. Not good! It took me months to recover from that."

"I approached a meeting with one executive as an informal chat. I was not as prepared as I should have been. He let me know it, and I have been overly prepared ever since."

"In a steering committee with multiple executives, I was walking through a solution to correct a problem that had a major impact on our schedule and budget. I had buy-in from my boss and my peers on what we were recommending. The meeting got derailed by one executive who wanted more context on the root cause of the problem. I had been out of the country and couldn't speak to the specifics he wanted around the situation that led to the problem. My credibility was shot at that moment, and it took an extremely long time to overcome it."

"I went to my first meeting expecting to be told what to do, rather than taking the executive an opinion and a recommendation. I lost the opportunity to be seen as someone who can understand a challenge and think through the best way to solve the challenge."

"I worked for a very volatile leader who tended to lose his temper in meetings when he didn't hear what he was looking for. My team went in with twenty PowerPoint slides and true to form, he exploded halfway through. He moved on to the next team. They put a single sheet of paper in front of him that summarized what they were going to recommend to him. He calmed immediately. I've never forgotten that contrast."

I hope the concepts ahead will help you avoid the frustration and the risks in high-level conversations. The key ingredients in our executive conversation framework answer the leaders' expectations, and hundreds of workshop participants and coaching clients have validated that it works. In fact, you'll find that the book actually follows this framework as well. Here's how:

At this point, I've put context around the topic of executive conversations. I've made the case for why the dilemma exists by sharing research and highlighting the pain points with survey results and anecdotes from both managers and executives. At this point, you should feel the dilemma is real. That was intentional. The flow of the book leads you to a clear need or gap to be solved around executive conversations.

Establishing what is happening and why it's happening is an essential part of the executive perspective. Executives need good context, and that's the most common element that managers leave out. Ultimately, over the first four chapters, I've led you to what needs to be solved. If I've done it well, you're now interested to know how I'll solve it with the core ingredients I referenced previously. It works well with executives, and I hope it's worked well with you.

In the chapters ahead, each of the core elements will be clearly identified. So, let's move forward with a solution that drives impact.

Section 2:

The Solution

5

The Bottom Line

"Make the bottom line your first line."

By far the most important element to develop for any executive meeting is a compelling message. The message drives home a clear *takeaway* and tells the executive what you want and the business outcome you can deliver.

From the moment you walk into an executive's office, the first thought on his mind is, "Why are you here? How is your topic relevant to me?"

In our workshops, managers role-play an upcoming executive conversation so they can apply our concepts to an actual meeting. In each program, we start by asking the managers to demonstrate how their meetings begin. Most managers state an objective for the meeting. Then, they jump straight into the details of the topic without telling the executive why the topic is relevant to him and to the business.

Consider this example:

"Thanks for your time today. Our topic is global marketing, and over the next thirty minutes, we want to share this year's plan with you."

The topic is clear, but an impatient executive has no idea why he should care about the global marketing plan. This meeting begins with the manager's objective, but it doesn't reveal a clear benefit to the business or the executive.

After hearing the first few minutes of any role-play, we ask three key questions:

- What is the topic of the meeting?
- What decision or input is the manager asking for?
- What is the benefit or outcome for the business?

Together, these elements create a compelling message. Great messages are delivered in one sentence and combine the concept of what you want and what's in it for both the executive and the business if you get it. One model for crafting messages is this:

If we (do this - the *ask* of the business), we will (get this - a measureable business outcome).

The *ask* of the business is an action or buy-in, and it may be specific to the executive or more general to the business. The measureable outcome helps the executive determine if the action is worth taking. Consider the following adjustment to the previous example:

"Our topic today is global marketing, and our message is this: By investing $4 million in our global marketing strategy, we will gain visibility in Central America and increase our sales leads by 25% this year."

If you're the executive sitting across the desk, isn't the message much more compelling than the overview statement? The message gives the executive what he needs:

- The topic of the meeting: global marketing.
- The *ask*: $4 million investment.
- The return or benefit: visibility in Central America and 25% increase in leads.

Most managers see an example of a compelling message and worry that it's too risky, and it is a little risky. It states a measurement that you may not want to be accountable for achieving. Nevertheless, accountability is the cost of entry to an executive-level conversation. You could state a less compelling message, such as:

"By supporting our global marketing strategy, you will gain visibility in Central America and increase our sales leads."

Then, the executive is going to quickly interrupt the meeting and ask how much of an investment you need and what you believe the impact will be. Executives typically hijack meetings because they need clear measurements and expectations in order to decide whether the business should follow your recommendation. Without the measurements, it's just an overview discussion. And most executives would say, "If you aren't ready to commit to the costs of the *ask* and the impact of the investment, then you're not ready to meet with me."

A compelling message pushes the manager to put a stake in the ground and state the bottom line, which links what he wants with a business impact he can achieve. When done well, it establishes the manager's right to "lead" the conversation. The message sends a signal that you're clear about what you need or what you want to recommend and that you are willing to predict and prove a business outcome based on your recommendation. This solves the most common reason executives hijack meetings: they want to know what your point is. With a compelling message, you've already stated it.

In Chapter 2, I said that executives expect to get involved in the conversation within five minutes. Trying to find their role in the conversation is the second most common reason they interrupt. A compelling message also clearly defines their role. The executive understands from the *ask* what you want them to do or to support. So, they know from the start of the meeting that you want an action from them, and they will listen and participate with this action in mind.

Messaging is easiest when the topic is specific and the *ask* is clear, but not every executive conversation is about approving budgets or projects. Some meetings are quarterly reviews or project updates, and some meetings recommend stopping projects. However, all executive conversations still require a clear message and stated outcome for the business. Even the routine meeting shouldn't be approached as an overview or a summary; executives always want the *CliffsNotes* version of what you're doing. Give them the one key takeaway from the quarter: the "bottom line" strategy that worked well or what you need to solve as you move forward. Here are some examples of messaging from quarterly reviews with executives:

"By adjusting our spend next month, we should save 10% across the regions and stay in sync with our annual forecast."

"If we increase our resources by 5% on Project XYZ, we can reduce downtime from our coding error and get back on track for the October release date."

"If we stay the course with our ABC campaign, you will see expected gains of 15% and new opportunities within ninety days."

"By eliminating our tracking tool, we expect a drop in enrollments next quarter, but we should see a 20% adjustment in profits by year end."

It isn't easy to sum up a quarter's work in one sentence. It takes effort to get the message right, and the message is exactly where you want to invest the effort. Here's why, according to the executives themselves:

"Meetings with me are productive less than 50% of the time if no outcome is stated."

"Managers can get so deep in the weeds or focused on tactics that they lose sight of why they're doing something."

"I need a compass for a meeting. If you don't know where we're going, then any road will get us there."

"In the shortest time possible, tell me why I'm there and what decisions I need to make."

"Be concise and connect your strategy and execution with priorities in the company."

"If you can't state a business benefit, then I can't figure out how you fit in my strategy."

"Don't bury the lead. I'm nervous about a meeting without a subject line."

"Keep it simple and make the ask."

"Give me the punch line quickly."

"Immediately explain how the topic will help us reach our goals."

"Have a clear point of view statement at the beginning of the meeting."

"Tell me why the topic is important to me and the company."

I could fill another ten pages with quotes from executives. We asked for insights on what they consider to be the important elements of a successful meeting and what it takes to capture their attention in a meeting. For an executive, these are one in the same: tell me what you need and how the business benefits from it. From the survey, 97% said the clear *takeaway* was the most important element.

A compelling message isn't just a test to see if you've done your homework. It helps an executive get to an outcome, which

LEADING
EXECUTIVE
CONVERSATIONS

"We put managers in these conversations all the time, and we do so very intentionally to get a look at how they show up. It is absolutely essential to promotion in our organization."

"I've got good instincts about people. I'll listen to others if my first impression is poor, but it will be hard to get back in front of me. If my impression is favorable, others can't talk me out of it."

"Remember that meeting with an executive is not a relationship – it's a transaction. They don't put a lot of thought into you; they just form an impression. If you show up positively, they will begin to put more thought into you, and that's how you'll get visibility in an organization."

All of the executives said they guard their own teams from senior-level exposure until they have confidence a manager will show up well. They do this because they know the manager won't get multiple opportunities, and they believe the manager is a reflection of their entire department. Therefore, the impressions the manager establishes have a direct impact on the executive who takes them to the meeting.

"I am very careful with someone who doesn't show up well. I intentionally limit their exposure to our leadership because their presence, or lack of it, is a reflection of my whole team."

"I took a manager into a meeting, and he kept his head in his notes the whole time. I noticed; my peers noticed; the manager was the only one who didn't notice. I took him to the meeting to establish his skills as an expert; he established that he didn't have the right to be there."

"I took a bright manager to a meeting with our CEO. I realized he was overwhelming the CEO with data points, and I nudged the manager in an attempt to help him read the room. I jumped in twice to help him, but he just couldn't see it. I wasn't surprised when the CEO pulled me aside at the end of the meeting and said, 'Don't bring him back.'"

"Impressions are like living things – they can change and ebb and flow. Good impressions can go downhill, and a lukewarm impression can shift and carry the day, but my impressions don't change 180 degrees."

As you can see from the quotes above, presence is the "hidden factor" in these meetings that moves initial impressions to lasting ones. In fact, seasoned managers learn that an effective style not only establishes a memorable impression, but also focuses the executive seated across the table.

12

Establishing
the Right to Be There

---

*"It takes a little courage to get a seat at the table; it takes
a lot of courage to lead the discussion."*

I have talked about the manager's role in high-level conversations and have offered insights and tools to help managers show up well in these meetings. Not surprisingly, executives themselves don't always show up so well either. They're busy, and it can be hard to shift their focus onto your topic and your takeaway.

A message and framework help this immensely, but your style can also help focus an executive. There's a concept that we call *settling*, and we demonstrate it in our workshops. We set up a roleplay and describe a scenario where the manager will be meeting with a top executive. As background, we tell the group that the executive has canceled this meeting twice already, so the manager has been delayed in their request to move an initiative forward, and they really need to get sign-off in this meeting. We pull someone from the class to sit in a simulated office, and we tell them that the executive is running fifteen minutes late for the thirty-minute meeting.

I play the role of the executive and rush into the office apologizing for the delay, but I tell the manager that we only have fifteen minutes because I'm needed in another meeting. The workshop participant who is playing the manager experiences the executive as distracted, rushed, and very uninterested in the topic at hand. Sound familiar? Most managers say, "Yes – that's exactly what happens to me!"

> "I had an executive who read emails the entire time I was talking to him. I didn't know whether to stop talking, keep talking, or pick up the pace, so I picked up the pace, and I think that was a big mistake."

> "I read their body language and always end up thinking I need to get through my thoughts faster."

> "I go into these meetings with my thoughts well organized, but I used to assume that the executive would want to lead the conversation. I would go in prepared to react to him rather than to lead him in a discussion. My manager told me that this made the executive feel I wasn't prepared at all."

> "I've been in three executive meetings where the time was cut short. I tried to condense the discussion, but I know I got flustered trying to reorganize my flow of ideas on the spot."

> "It's bizarre; I'm prepared before the meeting starts, and then I'm totally at a loss once it gets underway!"

"I had an executive who became my mentor because he was honest with me. In my first meeting with him, I moved really fast and plunged into detail. He stopped me about ten minutes into the meeting and said, 'It's clear that you're passionate. I want to believe you, but I have no idea what you just said.' He gave me the gift of insight, and I learned quickly to slow my pace and be more intentional with my thoughts."

"It's intimidating to sit across the desk from someone who seems so confident. It rattles me and seems to jumble my thoughts. I wish I could just relax in this setting."

In each of these comments, it's evident that the executive's presence is impacting the manager, and in the role-play I described earlier, that's exactly what we're trying to illustrate. While it's critical to have presence in these meetings, managers need to be aware that executives will unintentionally impose their styles on you.

In the workshop role-play, we ask the manager to describe how the executive comes across. As I stated earlier, the manager will use words like distracted, uninterested, and rushed. Then, I ask the manager to describe how they felt during the role-play. Most find it unnerving, uncomfortable, and rushed. They feel that they rambled, spoke very fast, and lost their train of thought.

In the role-play, I'm able to demonstrate that the manager began to speed up or get flustered because of the executive's style. This is an example of how the executive imposes his style on someone else. It isn't intentional. Executives are just busy and often distracted by other priorities, so it can be difficult to get them focused on the discussion at the beginning.

Messaging is the tool to remedy this, but it also requires that a manager's style be very settled, intentional, and composed as the meeting begins. In our role-play, we repeat the exercise, and I swap places with the workshop participant. They play the role of the executive and mimic what they've seen me do in the first role-play. They come into the simulated meeting rushed and distracted by things on their desk. As the manager, I'm able to pull their focus into the conversation and use my style to bring a sense of calm to the interaction. This time, I ask the participant to describe how they experienced the manager, and they say the manager (my role) seemed very intentional and focused. "Your pace was deliberate, and you seemed to wait for me to get a little more settled as well." Then, I ask what the impact of the manager's style was on their attempt to play the rushed executive. The participant usually says, "I was drawn to you when you paused and waited for me to focus on you. I immediately relaxed and actually heard you better." Managers learn that it takes both content and presence to establish the right to be there.

During the interviews for the book, I heard several stories from executives that reinforced this. One executive told me that she once interviewed for a senior role and happened to know the woman who had been in the role previously. As she talked to the CEO about what he needed, he made a comment about the other woman not being a good fit for him. The woman who was interviewing asked him why her predecessor wasn't a good fit because she had thought her predecessor did very well with the job. The CEO said, "Well, she may be good in her field, but she always seemed intimidated by me. You can't do a good job on my team if you're intimidated. You won't give good feedback."

It's your style or presence across the desk that establishes those impressions. Another executive told me that he observes his top leadership team in meetings with young managers all the time.

> "The managers just miss the signals of the executives who are moving quickly. It isn't personal; the executives are just jumping from one setting to the next and moving quickly through a day because they just aren't focused yet. Managers take it personally and get flustered quickly. It would help immensely if the managers understood the concept of getting settled and could learn to focus an executive, rather than taking on the rapid pace themselves."

Your ability to appear settled and intentional establishes your right to be there and actually helps the executive focus on you. You will also find it helpful to send the right amount of pre-read materials before the meeting takes place, so let's look at what executives want and what they review before most meetings.

13

Preview vs. Pre-work

"It doesn't take much preparation if you plan to send me everything."

As we started interviewing executives and managers about executive-level conversations, one of the top questions on my mind was what kind of pre-work executives like to receive. For years, I've heard managers talk about preparing decks to send to leaders in advance. I've reviewed many of these decks with managers and have always felt it was just too much material to go through. But, managers are adamant that pre-work is required, and they send an average of twenty to thirty slides as a pre-read.

In recent years, I've paid more attention to those decks in the hands of executives. I frequently ask, "What do you do with this?" And, the most common reply is, "Nothing. That's just too much information." In many of the interviews, the topic of pre-work and pre-reads sparked the interest of executives, and several of them wanted to show me the amount of material they receive prior to meetings. It's a point of frustration, and it often doesn't seem to be doing what managers hope it will do.

Perhaps the most perplexing part is that managers think they're doing what executives require. When I asked executives about the large decks, they said,

> "I never asked for a full PowerPoint deck. Who has time to review that? I just want the salient points summarized so I can be ready for the meeting."

Their reaction uncovered an interesting question: Who **is** asking for the decks?

Across all of our research, this is an open item. There's no question that executives expect to receive something in advance of the meeting. In fact, our research proved that they believe managers should spend more time getting ready for the meeting than managers themselves think is necessary. See examples of preparation for executives in the Resources section.

But, as one executive said, "100 slides of explanation is a data dump," and they've been pretty clear that they don't want that.

This is aligned with the confusion about wanting you to be prepared to answer questions, but also keep the conversation at a high level. Executives feel the same way about preparation. They want you to be well informed and up-to-date across the organization on your topic, but they don't want to wade through all of that to get ready for the meeting.

In fact, many organizations go to great lengths to try and reduce the amount of information shared. Through the years, we've seen restrictions on slide count and structure around pre-reads. Many companies use a plan on a page for operational reviews, or a SWOT diagram to compare new opportunities. Most recently, there's been interest in materials that resemble more of an executive overview. Amazon made this format popular by sharing their discipline of beginning every staff meeting with thirty minutes of silence while everyone reads the pre-work.

Through the years, I've worked with many groups on fitting their ideas into boxes, squares, columns, and even circles. It's pretty common for managers to put a lot of time and effort into fitting their ideas into a restrictive format, and they express a lot of frustration in what they often feel is a useless exercise. Nevertheless, executives are unapologetic about the requirement. "It's well worth the time managers put into our framework because it forces them to get their thoughts focused and more concise around their topic."

And, ironically, if managers are concise with their ideas, the ideas are much more likely to get pushed up through the ranks and show up in someone else's deck.

Executives are consistent in their desire to review something before meetings, but there is some variation in what they actually want. Here's what several executives said they like to see:

> "I like a strategy document, not a PowerPoint deck. This shows me that you're ready for the meeting."

> "I asked a manager for an executive summary. The deck I received suggested he didn't really know what that was. I

worked with him to produce a structure for this, and it has really helped him understand how to structure our meetings and the materials I like in advance."

"Establish game rules up front. It always helps you show up better."

"Decks are a crutch and a comfort for the manager, not me."

"I like to see ideas on paper so I can see how you think different elements of an idea come together."

"I like two pages as a pre-read; I won't take a meeting without it."

The challenge for managers is that while the framework of the meeting is pretty universal for an executive audience, one size doesn't fit all when it comes to pre-reads. My advice is to get a sense of each executive's preference, and executives agree with me. In fact, well over 70% of them thought you should discuss your agenda in advance of the meeting with your boss or a peer to get feedback before meeting with the executive.

"Ask my direct reports about my style. You'll learn how to handle my questions."

"Precondition your agenda with a coach or another manager who has met with me recently."

"Discuss the meeting agenda and takeaway with your boss before you meet with me."

"Know what we've done on this topic before as a company."

"You should have reviewed all existing material within our company on this topic before you come to me."

While that may feel like a lot of work for one meeting, the more seasoned managers say they do it.

In interviews, most managers talked about trying to understand the executive's perspective well in advance of the meeting. They ask managers who have attended recent meetings with the executive for a sense of what's on his mind. They ask the executive's chief of staff or administrator about current topics and priorities. They also say that they take time to think about the data points they're taking in and what they really mean for the business. If they're going to show an executive that sales are down by 20%, they've learned to know more than just the data point. They'll think about what the data point will mean to the company and what the executive is likely to ask them. As we discussed in Chapter 8, they will give thought to how the data impacts an outcome or a trend within the company; it isn't the number itself that's important. It's what the number may be an early indicator of that drives the executive.

When I work with managers on pre-reads, I'm checking to be sure that the meeting overview covers what the executive will need to know to make a decision. As a few executives said in the interviews, "What would we need to know to be the best we can be during your meeting?"

While this step may be more fluid, don't skip it. Several managers said that they led meetings with no pre-reads because they weren't sure what the executive wanted. That's a mistake. They all expect something and will view a manager with a well-written summary as someone who is prepared.

Our framework is a good starting point and easily adjusts to a one page format as outlined in the Resources section of the book. I've worked with many executives to design a template that they like, and it often begins with our meeting framework.

In outline form, we state the message and then give three key bullets to overview the Situation, Solution, and Impact/Next Steps. The pre-read is a condensed and simpler way to show them what you will prove in the meeting.

In PowerPoint form, we devote one slide to define the topic and message/takeaway, and then we use one slide to cover each key component: Situation, Solution, and Impact/Next Steps. If you're using slides instead of an outline, remember that slides tie to sub points. So, don't list three bullets on a slide as you would the outline. Instead, pick one of the points and illustrate it on the slide. The other points will be part of the live discussion.

This may help you determine which format is best for your meeting. If you have compelling data points to support the discussion, you may prefer to send a chart to show the comparison in advance. If the conversation is more about trends or expectations for performance, you'll build a better story with an outline. See the Resources section for examples of both formats.

The bottom line is that most executives will want something in advance, but they aren't going to work hard to digest what you send them. They just want to see the storyline and what you're asking them to do, so put away the thirty-page slide decks. They aren't reading them, and it may be creating more frustration than you realize. Keep it to just one or two pages, or four slides. Frame the point of the meeting and the key elements that you're bringing for discussion. Ultimately, they agreed to the meeting for the conversation more than the data points.

I heard a White House executive summarize it well when he was asked about the amount of pre-work required in the White House. I've always remembered his quip, "We call it a briefing for a reason; if we wanted a lot of verbiage, we would call it a longing."

That says it all.

14

The Remote Meeting

"I'm just like everyone else. If you aren't sitting across from me, you don't have my full attention."

Remote meetings are on the rise, and more and more managers are finding that their high-level conversations are with an invisible audience. The rise in popularity is all about convenience, cost savings and the ability to connect people who are not in the same location. But, remote meetings don't work to the advantage of the manager. And, that's because it's harder to reach outcomes.

In every workshop we lead, managers ask for tips on how to handle remote conversations. Questions can range from one-on-one meetings to more formal presentations. My first point of clarification is that "remote meetings" itself is a generic term. There are many different types of remote meetings, and they all require different mediums and different techniques.

We think of these meetings in three categories: Conference Calls, Video Conferences and Webinars. The chart below describes the difference in the mediums and the ideal size and format of each.

CONFERENCE CALLS	VIDEO CONFERENCES	WEBINARS
• **Format:** Audio only	• **Format:** Telepresence/ Virtual in-person meeting	• **Format:** Visuals lead with remote narrator
• **Purpose:** Discussion and resolution on timely issue or opportunity	• **Purpose:** Interactive discussion to get others engaged in initiatives	• **Purpose:** Train and educate or high-level keynote
• **Ideal Size:** 4-6 people	• **Ideal Size:** 5-10 people	• **Ideal Size:** More than 10 people
• **Replaces:** Phone call	• **Replaces:** Live meeting	• **Replaces:** Formal presentation

Our topic is high-level, one-on-one conversations. Those conversations can shift to a conference call format effectively, but it comes at a price for a manager. Executives admit it's difficult to keep their attention in a remote setting, and they multi-task just like everyone else does. You definitely have to work harder to keep the listener engaged. Even if you have good facilitation skills, the worry is that you won't be as memorable as you are in person. Without non-verbal expressions that are necessary for connection, it can be difficult to truly engage the listener.

My advice to managers is to make sure the remote interaction isn't the only interaction. In Chapter 11, I wrote about the power of presence and how quickly executives form impressions. Those impressions are strong and lasting. At least half of their impression is based on physical presence such as how you use your body and how the audience sees you. For most of us, this visual part of presence is hard to replace. If your conversation is a virtual one, make it a point to meet the executive in person. The sooner the face-to-face meeting comes after your conversation, the better.

In fact, managers who work in the same physical space as the leaders they interact with are at an advantage. Physical presence accounts for more than half of the impact of impressions, and it's more memorable. If you work remotely, you should make it a point to be in the home office several times a year. Most remote workers tell me they do that, but not all managers take advantage of these visits. Use this time wisely. Schedule five-minute introductory meetings. Walk the halls. Meet the executive assistants. The more people you know, the easier it will be to schedule meetings and keep your name top of mind, even though your physical presence may not be.

I've also encouraged many managers to request a videoconference format for a remote meeting. Many companies have added this capability, and it makes a difference in listener participation and meeting outcomes. I am encouraging senior executives to put the capability in their offices. Most have cameras attached to a desktop or built into a laptop. The capability is there, but the use of the technology still requires prompting. Don't be afraid to ask an executive assistant about this possibility. Many executives say they're happy to do it; they just don't think about it. On the contrary, if you're talking to an executive who's on the go instead of sitting in the office, it is often too cumbersome to use.

Our coaching around remote meetings focuses on three P's: Preparation, Participation, and Presence.

PREPARATION

Preparation for a remote audience takes more effort, but managers often think this setting allows them to be more informal and less prepared. Don't fall into that trap! If it's difficult to keep their attention, you're going to need to work extra hard to make the conversation interactive. A pre-read will be critical for these conversations because it will serve as a guide to help the executive follow your thoughts. You can use our framework as the pre-read, but be careful to keep the focus of the meeting narrow. Executives say that when remote conversations exceed twenty minutes their attention starts to wane, so you won't be able to cover as much ground.

As you organize your thoughts for this meeting, pay attention to the message and takeaway to be sure they're possible to prove in a shorter format. Here's an example of how to narrow the message for a remote setting.

Topic: Quarterly Projections

In-Person Meeting Message: By doubling our promotion spend, we should be able to increase interest in our new device and lift sales by 20% this year.

Remote Meeting Message: By adding a contest to our promotion budget this quarter, we expect to see a 5% lift in sales.

If I'm meeting with you in-person, I'll cover our plans for the total spend and show you what the new device can do in twelve months' time. In a remote meeting, I'll focus only on the quarter and a specific promotion we want to add. If all of my meetings have to happen remotely, I'll schedule more than one meeting and divide the annual plan into segments which will be easier to digest.

If the executive wants all of the information in one remote meeting, be sure that you send comprehensive pre-work and an outline to help you manage their focus and attention. Plan for breaks during the call where you can ask for feedback and buy-in.

Topic: Project Funding

In-Person Meeting Message: If we invest an additional $500,000 in our analytics tool kit, we can expand our view of customer behaviors and launch segmentation campaigns within thirty days.

Remote Meeting Message: By running a ten-day trial, we can test our hypothesis about customer behaviors and understand how to expand our analytics tool kit.

Again, the in-person meeting message is broader and recommends expanding the analytics approach to get richer data on customer behaviors for segmentation campaigns. In a virtual meeting, I'm focused on the first step of the expanded approach which is a ten-day trial. In this case, I'll conduct the trial and then have a follow-up conversation to discuss expanding our analytics approach based on the trial results. If I were meeting in-person, I could probably get the funding and the trial out of the same discussion.

Without a visual presence, the listener begins to rely on other components of the conversation for impressions. The document sent in advance says more about you in a remote setting than it might if the executive were to see you walk into his office.

PARTICIPATION

Participation is critical from the moment the conversation begins. To lead an in-person meeting, we tell managers to state the message/takeaway, state the overview for context and to help understand the flow of the conversation, as well as to help steer the conversation into the External Perspective of the Situation before soliciting input from the executive. This provides context about the meeting and the topic.

The remote meeting is different. In this setting, executives say listening is participating, and you'll have to allow for a more dynamic back and forth with each step of your content journey. You'll have to replace non-verbal nods with a verbal "yes" or "I agree" in order to know that the executive hears the meeting objective and understands the message/takeaway you want to achieve.

Soliciting verbal response can be challenging and takes practice. To force interaction and participation, I would write possible questions on the conversation outline. Then, plan in advance where you will ask for a response. A silent listener doesn't indicate agreement; sadly, it often means they aren't fully listening.

PRESENCE

Remote conversations are harder and so is establishing presence. As I mentioned earlier, physical presence and the ability to own a room by imposing a settled presence doesn't exist. In remote conversations, the voice has to establish all the attributes of presence. The impact of your voice on impressions goes from 38% to 85%. It makes sense; it's all you've got.

In Chapter 11, I gave high-level concepts of presence: Confidence, Commitment, and Connection. The voice is best at Commitment and putting energy and effort behind your words. In a remote setting, the voice must also establish an impression of Confidence and Connection.

In our Executive Presence workshops, we conduct an exercise that simulates a remote experience. The purpose is to show participants how much effort it takes to get someone's attention using only your voice. The exercise asks participants to stand on opposite sides of the room, facing away from each other, so they can only hear what is said. Without exception, it is always more challenging than the managers imagine to be clearly understood. When they give each other feedback on the voice impression, it's almost always tied to articulation and projection rather than volume. Here are a few key coaching notes to power up your voice for a remote call:

Pace & Pause: Your voice pace can establish confidence and credibility. If you have a tendency to talk fast or to ramble a bit with your thoughts, you lose this attribute. Your goal should be to sound intentional and deliberate with pace. Some managers find it helpful to script the first portion of the meeting and mark it for pause to be sure the voice pace establishes the right to lead the conversation. Doing this helps you come across as if you have a well thought out plan and direction.

It also addresses the executive's concern, should this person be talking to me? And, does this person have the ability to lead our conversation?

Energy & Effort: It's easy to confuse a fast-paced speaker with an energetic one because we often think that someone who talks fast has a lot of energy. In order for me to feel that the topic matters to you, you're going to have to articulate well. The easiest way to think about articulation is the idea of getting the whole mouth involved as you speak. We help managers experience articulation by making them count from one to five. In our simple exercise, you count out loud and then you count without sound. You can quickly feel how much harder you work when the whole mouth is involved.

Speaking with the whole mouth or articulation creates energy behind your words and communicates your thoughts clearly and crisply. A simple way to power up the voice is to assume the remote audience is twice the size that it actually is. So, if you're talking to one person, assume you're talking to two. If there are three listeners, assume there are six. That helps most managers bring more energy to the conversation.

Project to Connect: Connection is the hardest concept to establish remotely. Both of the concepts already mentioned contribute to connection. An intentional pace and increased effort behind the words captures the attention of the listener. You can also improve the warmth in the voice by projecting the voice forward. We do this naturally when we focus on people as we speak to them, but often in a remote setting the head is down reading over notes or talking to a PowerPoint deck instead. Be sure to keep the head up and send the voice forward. Call centers train to this element when they tell operators to smile when they speak.

Virtual meetings have less impact, but they can reach good outcomes. This is a different skill, and you should incorporate the three P's to be sure you can achieve results from a remote executive conversation.

Section 5:

The Complexities

15

Building Consensus

"Small meetings are career makers and big meetings are career breakers."

The challenges inherent to executive conversations become more complex when there are more executives involved. If it's hard to keep one executive focused, imagine what it's like to have five of them sitting around the table. Chances are the conversation will get derailed, probably more than once.

It's essentially like trying to have five separate conversations within one conversation. In fact, everything that makes one executive predictable in establishing value and business outcomes goes a little sideways when multiple executives are involved.

And, that's because they all value different things and make decisions to drive different business outcomes. The next chapter will talk further about their different perspectives. In this chapter, I want to focus on building consensus and pre-selling ideas to a high-level audience.

The first realization is about outcomes. This isn't an audience that will take a recommendation and rubber stamp it. If they do, consider that a "once in your career" kind of discussion. With multiple executives, managers shouldn't look for a quick sign-off. Think more in terms of handing them an idea that they will scuff up. You can be vested in getting to an outcome, but don't get wound too tight in exactly how you will get there.

> "A lot of managers come to our team with great pride and joy. They've toiled away on a recommendation and present it with a great sense of accomplishment. But, it is rarely taken as presented. Executives start the conversation with what should be modified."

Knowing that they will stretch, pull, and modify the recommendation, you need all the insights you can get before the group conversation takes place. This is where the manager's approach to meetings and the executive's approach to meetings often differ. When executives bring ideas to their own peer group, they rarely introduce an idea to the group before vetting it outside the room with these same individuals. They pre-sell ideas and are well prepared to make sure that any recommendation or direction has each executive's perspective taken into account. And, if they can't meet everyone's needs, they are upfront about the trade-offs and compromises that will have to be made from different areas.

It takes a lot of work, but it reduces surprises. More importantly, it's the way things get done at an executive level.

Managers don't really do that with their peer group. The accepted practice in group discussions is to bring new ideas to a team. Recommendations are hashed out as a team, and managers handle questions and concerns with everyone and across all departments. It may be because the executives' universe is so much broader that it would be almost impossible to answer concerns of an entire function area while keeping the attention of five other function areas with different concerns.

At a senior level, consensus is built before the group conversation ever takes place. That's how you avoid a career breaker. When I asked senior leaders about this concept, they agreed that their practice is to pre-sell ideas before meetings. They were also a little surprised to remember that they didn't always do it that way. Many admitted they haven't coached their own teams to do it well.

> "I agree the pre-sell approach is very common at the senior level; most managers haven't been coached to do it."

One executive shared his own experience in learning this idea the hard way.

> "I had my moment of visibility with the senior leadership team, and I was scheduled to make a recommendation on a mature product in our offerings. I reviewed my presentation with my boss and showed him my plans to recommend that we drop one product and invest rapidly in the promotion of another. The majority of my presentation was about investing in that new opportunity. He quickly let me know that I hadn't spent any time addressing the trade-offs that the abandoned product would mean for each member of the ex-

ecutive team. And, that's when I knew I was missing their perspectives."

You have to consider getting to consensus as part of your overall strategy. Here's how you do it:

Executive Sponsorship: Start with your boss and think through the executive team and their interest in your topic. While you may not get to all of the executives before the meeting, you should prioritize your pre-sell work based on those who are most impacted by your topic. So, prioritize the key stakeholders.

One executive talked about being used as a resource to vet ideas for the CEO. She, like other leaders, is cautious about what she lends her name to and what she agrees to support. Leaders understand the value of having support in the organization, but they want to attach their support to winning concepts. The visibility and exposure is greater with a full senior team. Make sure you can deliver on the ideas that an executive agrees to sponsor.

Gather Background: Talk to seasoned managers in each executive's organization and gain insights and uncover possible roadblocks for your topic. Find the managers who have the most to gain or lose from your idea. They probably have influence over the executive's perspective and can help you understand the impact and offer possible compromises.

Pre-Sell Your Ideas: With your manager's help, you need to meet with the key stakeholder(s). Map out a plan to put yourself or your manager in front of the executive(s). This meeting should be positioned as seeking input and reaction to a pending recommendation. In the meeting, probe to understand what the executive values in the recommendation and what she sees as roadblocks. Talk through how those elements can be solved. Leave with a clear sense of what it would take for her to support the idea.

The most critical part is to understand their perspective and capture the trade-offs they would be willing to endure to get to the outcome.

Modify the Recommendation: Once you have input, you need to rethink how the recommendation will be presented. It may be options that show the trade-offs across divisions. A group of executives are good with choices. No more than three, well-vetted options that give them an understanding of what they trade-off with each.

My experience is that a group of executives interact better when reviewing options versus a single recommendation. This gives you the flexibility to show alternatives that favor different perspectives. You need to be prepared to recommend the option you think would be best to pursue, but also be open to input that might steer you in a different direction. Remember this is a group that plans to scuff up your recommendation.

Emphasize the Situation: As you organize your ideas into the framework from Chapter 6, you want to focus heavily on the Situation element in Chapter 7. One of the hardest concepts for managers to communicate to executives is their common ground on a topic. It is rarely in the Solution. And, that's because they bring different perspectives and drive different objectives in the company. The options you present in your recommendations will likely compromise one or more of them in some way.

They do find common ground in the Situation. You can reach consensus around the external perspective on your topic and why you believe action or thought is needed. Expand the time you spend discussing the Situation to be sure the executive group is comfortable with the context and aligned with solving some element of your topic. Once they understand and buy in to the need for a solution, they will be more flexible in the give and take of getting to a solution.

I've also had many managers say that a well-positioned Situation helped them to keep bringing the executive discussion back to common ground and guide the executives to compromise.

As one manager shared, "The issue I took to our senior leadership team was contentious. There just wasn't going to be a solution that they all liked. But, when I started with the Situation and gave them good reason to understand why a change was needed, I found that they used those key points to push each other to resolution."

It's been said that executive communication is 80% facilitation and 20% content. The information in the Situation helps a manager set up common ground and drive facilitation.

As I talked to executives about conversations with their peer group, they all agreed that building consensus was paramount. Their best advice was to talk to others who have led presentations and conversations with a senior team and learn from their experiences. All agreed that this isn't an environment where you want to show up as if you've never done it before.

As we teach these concepts, managers often complain that it's a lot of work to prepare for these discussions. They're right, it is. But, remember this is a high visibility moment and an opportunity that will have an impact on your career. Treat it as such.

When a group of executives come together, you have the full attention of the company sitting in front of you. One consulting firm calculated that pulling together five C-level leaders from a large company costs $30,000/hour. Make sure the time you take up is well worth it.

16

Know Your Audience

"One manager came into my office with a thirty-slide PowerPoint deck, and I knew immediately that he hadn't done his homework. Anyone on my team could have told him that he'd never get past slide three."

While asking for background information about an executive's idiosyncrasies may feel like water cooler gossip, it's a step that most executives agree you should take. They recognize that they have different approaches, and they would rather not have to groom the entire company to fall in line with them. Learn from others, they say.

In our workshops, we help managers do just that. When we customize a program for a company, we include an exercise that allows managers to share their experience of interacting with key executives. The purpose is to capture how executives like to receive information and the manager's experience of how they listen and what they value. In some cases, managers have been able to point their colleagues to people who interact frequently with a particular executive and often have his ear. This may be a chief of staff role or a seasoned manager who has become a confidant. Either way, it's an individual who can provide exceptional perspective about the executive.

As I begin coaching sessions with executives, I always discuss the profiles of their key audiences. This helps me understand where they are strong in communication and where they may have gaps. It also gives me insight into how well they have focused on the needs of different audiences.

When I work with managers who are just beginning to get C-level exposure, I help them build out a profile of each executive on the leadership team. The idea is to coach them on learning the different expectations each leader will bring to conversations.

Over the years, I've learned this myself in coaching across the C-suite in hundreds of companies. While your company is unique in the marketplace and the strategies that a team may be driving, the function areas look pretty similar from one company to the next. So, a CFO in one company is often looking at similar things as the CFO of another company. I see it in their presentations and communications.

At the risk of oversimplifying, I often describe to managers how I see the C-level roles. These are seasoned leaders who are driving a defined set of goals and strategies to reach those goals. While their peers have knowledge of their goals, each executive is pretty autonomous in how they get there. And, they spend a good part of their time exploring and evaluating choices they can make to reach those goals. Every day, they consider choices that may compromise one initiative to accelerate another. The more you know about their goals and strategies, the easier it is to align with them.

Consider the following priorities and perspectives when communicating with some of the common C-level roles.

CEO: By function, this leader runs the team and is the one who truly owns the overall company direction. His most important audience is his Board, and he invests a lot of time communicating to this audience.

His perspective is usually external. He values concepts and insights into competitors and market trends. Most of his meetings with managers will include one of his function leaders, so you will often balance two perspectives in these conversations.

The common mistake in conversations with the CEO is that he is usually thinking six months ahead of what the business is actually doing. Not always, but often. So, managers can be surprised to learn that the CEO isn't on top of what closed in sales last week or the challenge a group is having with an IT implementation. He will always be interested in how an idea rolls up to overall company direction. Pay attention to what this leader has said in all-hands meetings and external communication. It will be good insight into his priorities.

CFO: More often than not, CFOs are sitting at the table when leaders make decisions about business strategies, long before the financial implications are concrete. While their career journey has led them to shift perspective from a financial one to a broader business outlook, remember where they came from. They still consider the holistic impact of numbers. So, not only revenue earned but also expenses incurred. Their level of detail varies widely from one personality to the other, but they have a hard time buying into anything if the math doesn't make sense.

The CFO is often described by managers as a roadblock to approvals. That may be the case, but it's often for good reason. The budget and plan for the current year reside in the CFO's function area. She has a lot at stake. While many of the other leaders will be enthusiastic about investing for next year's reward, this leader will push to be sure the current reality isn't compromised. As long as you understand that perspective and have considered the implications, you can get the CFO on board.

COO: This function doesn't exist in every company, but when it does, it represents the officer who takes responsibility for the day-to-day operations of a company. By function, they may have divisions reporting into them or other function areas. When the COO role exists, it allows the CEO to worry less about how the company delivers products and service every day. The COO is usually focused on leveraging and scaling ideas and minimizing impact. He may represent the largest employee group, so any communication to him should consider such things as implementation and business interruption.

CMO: The marketing function has transformed in recent years. Companies are positioning themselves and their products very differently than they have in the past. This leader got out from under the sales function by bringing new measurements and analytics to the leadership table. While closely aligned with sales, this officer is tasked to identify trends and measure customer engagement. She owns the customer experience more fully than she has before. You can tell a lot about this leader by how her function is organized. Marketing departments vary widely in their focus and their expertise. But, chances are, if you have an idea or project that will impact customer awareness and engagement, this leader will be intrigued.

Don't take this leader for granted. While she likes new ideas, she is also keenly aware of risks associated with not hitting metrics. She is no longer just supporting the front of the customer experience; she tracks the experience all the way to outcomes. Look for thought leadership from this executive. Find out what she has said about future direction and the marketing spend to align with it.

Division Presidents: These roles are the most autonomous after the CEO and may actually be run as separate companies. They care about what impacts their division and often not much else. That's not being short-sighted; most of them run big entities and have many of the peer functions within their own organizations. So, while they're interested in what the CMO may be doing for the company as a whole, they're more interested in what their marketing officer is doing to drive visibility. Their strategies can operate on a short timeframe as they are working hard to deliver on results. Their perspective may shift quarter to quarter depending on how their performance is to date. Pay attention to what they're doing and modify communication and recommendations accordingly.

One division president shared an experience of being asked by an IT manager for a $250,000 investment only one week after he had announced layoffs. Needless to say, that was a short conversation.

A pet peeve I've seen from this group is when a manager positions a project to division presidents collectively. The assumption is, "That manager thinks we're all alike." They feel strongly that they aren't. While they respect referrals and ideas from one another, they rarely believe that "one size fits all" is the best approach. The hardest communication with these leaders involves recommending a universal approach or a streamlined process. In fact, in some companies these leaders compete with each other.

This is a good example of where consensus building will be critical as will understanding the unique challenges and direction of each division.

Beyond the C-Suite: Certainly, not every executive you meet with will be C-level. However, even those one to two levels below the C-suite align their perspective and priorities with the top function leader. Usually, the higher the leader is in the organization, the broader their perspective is.

This chapter isn't meant to be a comprehensive profile of all the C-level functions in a company. You can learn a lot more about your executives from within your own company rather than from me. The overview is simply to get you thinking about why their perspectives differ so much. It's because their functions do. To be good at what they do, they stay focused on what the business is counting on them to deliver. If you invest the time to understand their perspective, you'll gain confidence in your ability to align with them.

17

Working Through a Middleman

"Five heads aren't always better than one, but you often have to deal with them anyway."

One common point of discussion in our workshops revolves around working through a middleman. The more experienced managers say their frustration isn't the senior executive, but their own boss who can get in the way when they are trying to lead a conversation or gain approval for a recommendation.

The direct boss almost always goes to these meetings with you, and he or she can be a disruptor. They seem to add points that aren't relevant which sidetracks the conversation. Some managers say it's hard to show up well with them in the room. Many feel the boss is trying to take credit for their hard work; others say the boss just wants to look good in front of the senior executive.

Occasionally, someone will speak up in the workshop and say, "Just go around them! Don't tell them about the meeting." From my experience, that is very risky advice. Here's why:

I coached one seasoned manager who was frustrated with his boss. He felt he had a good relationship with his boss's boss, the executive two levels above him, but was convinced that his manager was incompetent and had decided to keep her out of the loop. In the six months I worked with him, I cautioned him against this exclusive approach, and told him he really needed to keep his manager in the loop. While I thought the access to the senior leader was great, I knew he needed to keep his manager informed or he would experience repercussions from these on-going skip-level conversations.

I guess he didn't believe me because he continued to go around his boss and to seek approval for projects from the senior leader without gaining her buy-in first. It worked in the short-term. He got a lot of visibility with the leader and a lot of support for his project. But, when both the senior leader and his manager realized the chain of communication wasn't in place, it caused turmoil. His manager made some decisions without information from his initiative and it cost the company a lot of money. He was removed from the position six months later.

Another manager shared a story of her first experience with a senior leader in her company. She was three levels below the C-suite and got a call from a senior leader who wanted some information about an on-going project. She was pleased to be summoned to his office where she sat down with him and gave him an update on some of the challenges they were facing and steps they were taking to adjust the project. The meeting only lasted fifteen minutes, and she didn't think any more about it.

Within twenty-four hours, she was summoned to her manager's office and he was more than a little upset. He asked for clarification of the adjustments she had told senior leadership that *she* was making on the project and with a fair amount of energy explained the turmoil she had caused by giving out that information without letting him know about it.

While she didn't intend to keep it a secret, she also hadn't made it a point to tell her manager that she had the conversation. Unbeknownst to her, her manager was put on the spot the next morning when the senior executive called on him in a formal meeting and asked him to elaborate on the data points. Her manager wasn't prepared to do it and got caught off guard by the experience.

The middlemen in organizations call it the "no surprises" rule, and most leaders say it's better to understand this unspoken rule before learning it the hard way. Both managers in the stories above broke the rule. The first one broke it often enough to lose his job over it; the second manager just learned a hard lesson.

And, it's an important lesson to learn! Unless you report directly to someone in the C-suite, you will work through middlemen for these conversations. Even if your boss isn't in the meeting, she should always be informed of the conversation, in advance, if possible. There's no question that it makes the preparation more cumbersome, but it also protects you and everyone in between from the confusion or misdirection that comes when middlemen are left out of the communication loop. As one executive advised, "Cover your bases and all your bosses along the way."

It isn't always the managers' fault. In the second story, the manager was summoned to the executive's office. There's nothing wrong with that, and in fact, it's one of those visibility moments. But, senior leaders don't always appreciate the havoc they cause when they "ask for a quick update." You may have the full story and you may not. And, the challenge is you may not know the difference.

I've coached many top executives who encourage an open door policy. They walk the halls of their companies and they stand up in employee meetings and say, "I hope you'll stop by and let me know how things are going."

The intent is right on target, and walking the halls works. It brings an executive closer to what's happening within the company and gives them great insights into day-to-day wins and frustrations. But, everything they pick up along the way is quotable because it may be the only sound bite they get on a specific project or initiative. So, if you pass it along, be sure it's a sound bite that you're willing to back up. And, keep others in the loop on those conversations. If you've pulled the senior executive into an actionable item, chances are their action will impact many other managers along the way.

While it may sometimes seem cumbersome to build consensus with all the bosses along the way, they are a critical component of your success in high-level conversations. So, it's worth understanding their perspective on the role they play.

Most middlemen see themselves as conduits for your visibility to the C-level. Some are more than willing to highlight their team members and help you gain recognition and visibility for your work. Those are the middlemen who promote you. Some spend more time trying to limit managers in the spotlight because they worry that managers may not be ready for the heat and intensity. Those are the middlemen who shield you. And, many get caught in the middle of these two actions because they want visibility for their teams but they worry that the C-level executive will be a difficult audience.

I talked about this in Chapter 11. Visibility comes with risks, and the risks of a poor conversation reflect on both the manager and his manager, the middleman. So, the caution is warranted. Most middlemen want to be sure you're prepared for these conversations. To gain confidence and buy-in to your direction, they will review your materials, edit your slides and add note after note to your commentary. They are covering the bases, and some managers say they end up feeling very disheartened with the final product.

> "I felt good about my preparation for this conversation with the CMO until my boss reviewed my notes. Two days later, my well-thought-out conversation was diluted and so full of details that I didn't understand it myself."

That's where the quote at the beginning of the chapter comes into play. Five heads may not always be better than one, but you have to bring them into the loop. By understanding how to proactively do that, you can reduce some of the frustration experienced when your material gets diluted.

The most common reason that middlemen give for editing these conversations is that they don't hear a clear and compelling message and they can't follow the storyline. Sound familiar? Their sentiments are very similar to the executive perspective shared in Chapter 2. And that's a good thing. The middlemen present to the top level much more frequently. They know what it takes, and they are looking for those elements. Chances are if they are adding or editing information, it's for good reason.

But, they are rarely given the framework that I've shared with you in Chapter 6. Instead, they are handed a summary of a PowerPoint deck, and they are trying to look through data points and details to get to the storyline.

It's hard to do, and so they begin to add details to expand the storyline or to support what they think it might be. That's how information gets diluted, and managers end up with more information instead of less.

You should be seeking consensus on your storyline and not on your data points.

When given a level of detail, a middleman or any leader can think of more data points to add. We all look at details differently and there will always be endless perspectives to consider. In our framework, data points back up a higher-level storyline. And, that's where you want input and buy-in. If you can get consensus from the middlemen in your organization on what you're trying to accomplish and how you plan to lead the senior executive there, you'll find they allow you much more freedom to select the data points used to back-up your message.

I have seen this work time and time again. I'll work with a manager on a very high-level conversation, and I know that he needs to pre-sell his ideas to two middlemen along the way. We draft a one page summary of the framework to help him establish the message and the storyline in these early conversations. And, it works.

I spent one afternoon working with a product group that was struggling to get ideas through their SVP to the CTO for approval. I talked about this concept with them and explained that there was pressure on her as the middleman to be sure that the recommendations they were putting forward would be aligned with the CTO. They had worked for weeks on their decks, and they seemed to hit a stalemate with her.

We developed a simple, one page summary of the storyline for each manager. The group of five went back to her with those summaries, and they all got their message and direction approved. The group meeting with the CTO went beautifully and all projects moved forward.

You can stay true to what you know and minimize the dilution of your ideas, even with five heads in the discussion, but you have to be clear in positioning your message and the storyline to prove it out.

You may also find that your manager, or middleman, plans to play a role in the meeting. That can be disruptive if not planned for in advance. Most middlemen are best at setting some of the context in the Situation (see Chapter 7). Talk about this and plan for the middleman's role. The last thing you want is to be competing with your boss for air time in front of a senior leader.

Perhaps the best advice I can offer is dealing with the frustration expressed in the second paragraph. Managers worry that their boss wants credit for the project or will be focused on his or her own impressions with the senior executive. If that's true, it may not be a hurdle that you can overcome in every meeting. There are times that you will let your middleman down, and there are times that he will let you down. Don't worry too much about getting credit. Focus more on getting a seat at the table. Over time, if you can bring enough wins to the table, people figure out who is doing the great work.

18

Jekyll vs. Hyde in the C-Suite

"She went from a charismatic leader to a pit bull in less than fifteen minutes."

The opening quote is one I have remembered for a few years from an initial coaching session with a seasoned manager. The manager was a rising star in a company and because of her role in the legal department she had early access to the C-suite. One of the reasons she was working with me was to gain confidence in her meetings with the senior leadership team.

In our initial meeting, I asked her to talk about some of the executives and to share with me any concerns she had communicating with each of them. In short order, our conversation turned to the CEO. In her company the CEO was very charismatic, she was inspiring, compelling and very engaging with employee audiences. This manager was a bit in awe of her and couldn't wait to have more opportunities to be around this leader.

Her first meeting wasn't at all what she expected. The CEO was assertive in the conversation, pushed for information and immediately had the manager back on her heels with probing questions. The manager expected to have a conversation with the woman she observed who was driven by her passion, and instead, she was sitting across from a woman who was very focused on bottom-line costs and results. As she said, the manager felt that her charismatic leader went from a motivator to a pit bull in less than fifteen minutes. That may be a harsh label, but it is not an uncommon story.

In fact, it was after hearing a number of similar stories that I first realized the value we could bring to managers by helping them to understand the perspectives and personalities in the C-suite. If you don't sit in meetings with senior leaders often, it's easy to assume that the inspiration they use to rally a company might be the same approach they use to make the tough decisions. My experience is that most inspiring leaders were pretty tough and successful managers long before they gave their first inspirational talk.

The shift between inspiring people and running a business is a balancing act that most senior leaders pull off every day. In this chapter, I want to offer perspective on why managers may experience a shift in a leader's style and some ways that other managers have learned to navigate the shift from motivating to interrogating.

Most of my coaching clients are senior-level executives. Coaching relationships are focused on driving consistency and impact across a variety of audiences. Frequently, that coaching expands into coaching and training with others in a company. Since we experience both the manager's perspective and the executive's perspective, we understand the disconnect that managers are talking about when they first experience an executive's style.

Managers often share their impressions of executives with us. Most of the feedback we hear is good. Managers admire their executives' passion, they are on-board with the strategy and excited to be a part of the vision that the executives have set.

So, I try to bridge a little understanding of what it took for the executive to get there. It wasn't easy. It's hard to learn how to engage with an entire company. It takes a lot of effort to be inspiring and compelling. It takes practice and discipline to be able to set a high-level vision and drill down to a personal connection for every individual in a room, often in less than thirty minutes.

Most leaders are good communicators, but almost all of them seek help in mastering the power of impact. They also say they have to get "up" a bit and focus on being "in the moment" to pull that off.

When I hear managers say they want to sit across the table from that inspiring leader, I gently remind them that inspiring leaders spend more time being intense managers. Long before they developed the skills to inspire a group of thousands, they knew how to run a business and drive measureable outcomes.

One leader summed it up this way, "Those who report directly to me will tell you all of these meetings are intense. You don't show up unprepared more than once."

For most leaders, it's their natural style to be a little assertive in conversations and drill down to the details to get the information they need. They are visionary and will set a vision for what the business outcomes need to be. They'll also help pull every employee toward that vision as they unite the company on strategies and direction. But, if you are a part of smaller discussions around executing that vision, they will expect you to align yourself to the vision and present ideas that can deliver results.

Labeling an executive as Dr. Jekyll or Mr. Hyde is an extreme analogy. I used it as the title because most managers describe the comparison as extreme. It really isn't that dramatic of a shift. In fact, as you meet with a senior leader more frequently, you'll find they are consistent with their managerial style just as they are consistent as an inspiring leader. It is two different roles, which are going to show up a little differently in a small meeting than in a public setting.

I think most leaders realize they are seen differently, and many try to adjust a bit. As I said earlier, leaders describe being charismatic and inspiring as an energy level that they have to get "up" for a bit. While it's a great feeling to be in the auditorium when they deliver a keynote, you don't want to be the meeting that happens thirty minutes later. If it takes effort to get "up," it can also take a little time to wind down. It's hard to shift gears quickly, and the intensity and energy used for that keynote will linger awhile.

I have had some clients who learn to clear the calendar for a few hours after the "high energy" situations; others go for a run or workout. Still others only schedule time with the senior team who are used to the shift a bit more.

I talked about the ability of executives to focus and compartmentalize in Chapter 7; this is similar. The framework and focus that you bring to your meeting will help the executive transition from any previous meeting. But, regardless of what you follow on the calendar, managers should realize that the leader's intensity is not personal to you. It's almost always related to what came ahead of you. You are going to be shut down, cut off and frequently denied a request. But, that's the way they make business decisions.

Leaders carry a lot of weight on their shoulders. They need to make solid decisions that lead to business outcomes. There are consequences to every decision they make; it's pretty high stakes in their role. So, they push to eliminate gray areas and fully vet the consequences and opportunities.

Rather than bracing for the intensity as if you were headed into a strong wind, embrace it and go in with confidence behind your ideas and your recommendations. As one executive said,

> "I have one young manager in the IT department who keeps bringing me ideas. I'm sure I've turned down 95% of them. But, I love his tenacity. He reminds me of me, and I take every meeting he requests because he's the kind of guy who makes me a better leader."

I have also coached a number of managers who misread an executive's charismatic style and show up for "just a chat." Or, they hear "send me your thoughts," and they forward a rambling email. Remember the quote I shared in Chapter 3, "Don't confuse interactive with informal."

One seasoned manager was sent to me for coaching because the senior team didn't feel that he showed up with presence. He did need a little help in his personal style, but he needed more help in organizing his thoughts. When he got an email or voice mail from a senior leader asking for input, he just jotted down a few notes in response. One senior leader took his notes and sent him back a more formal executive summary with a note that said, "Try this." The manager brought it to a coaching session and asked me why I thought the executive had formatted his notes. I told him that the executive sent the information back that way because he doesn't think you know how to do it. Again, my message was don't mistake interactive with informal.

Another executive said, "I'm good with the drive by in the hall: a short conversation and a quick idea. But, I don't read anything more into it than that. If you are serious about a concept, I'm going to need to see that there's more to it."

Leaders can feel a little like Dr. Jekyll and Mr. Hyde as they go from a very public setting as a leader to a more private conversation as a manager. By understanding why the shift in style exists, you can adjust to it.

So, how do other managers adjust to a more assertive leader? Most learn from asking others what those smaller settings are like. This was feedback from the leaders themselves in Chapter 16.

In our workshops, we coach managers to impose their own settled style on an executive. With a more intentional pace and pause, you can help an executive settle into your meeting and focus on the discussion at hand.

Still others have become good at reading non-verbal communication. They pay attention to the executive's focus and pace as pleasantries are exchanged at the beginning of the meeting. They can tell by the executive's mannerisms when they are ready to settle into the conversation.

Most importantly, if you've done a good job of framing up the conversation in the pre-read materials, it will be much easier for the executive to focus on your message and the takeaway you're hoping to achieve.

I've talked a lot about how managers should prepare and show up for these meetings, and I'm sure it can feel as if all the responsibility for success is on the manager. That's not the case; executives don't always show up well for these meetings either. But, as I describe it in our workshops, that's not always easy for them to see.

They only see you and your reaction to their style as you sit across a conference table or desk. The trick is to recognize how they have shown up and to be adept at using your style and approach to help them adjust as needed. As one seasoned manager said,

> "You learn a lot about executives in closed-door meetings, and those impressions are seldom broadcast throughout the company. If you are new to these types of meetings, pay attention to how each leader operates and adapt quickly."

Well said.

19

What I Asked for Isn't What I Want

"When I can't get clarity on an issue, I will dive from ten thousand feet to ten feet looking for answers."

The quote above usually gets a lot of nods and chuckles from managers. In our workshops, I'm often asked why we don't coach senior executives to stay at ten thousand feet. We do, but as the quote suggests, it's human nature to start looking more deeply for details when you can't get the information you need.

I've said throughout the book that executives are predictable, and they stay consistent to the information they need. But, they can adjust altitudes quickly when they're trying to get context and understanding on an issue or opportunity. As managers have shared their experiences and as I have observed first hand, what they ask for isn't always what they want.

Let me share an example to illustrate how this can occur and then offer some ideas that we've found effective to keep the conversation at the right altitude.

Consider an executive who leads a growing, regional company with multiple product lines. He is considering expanding into a new market and thinks that it makes sense to phase the introduction of the products to drive brand recognition and volume in the early months. So, he wants to compare how the products performed in our markets and which drove the best brand recognition. He'll use this to think about how the company prioritizes the roll-out of products in the new market. To keep the example simple, I'll just call his products red, yellow, green, and blue.

As a manager you wouldn't know that he's white-boarded this concept in his office and has been thinking through several different scenarios that might make sense. He goes from his memory of what happened over the last two years, and he thinks that it makes sense for the red product to be the initial offering. In fact, based on some market data he's seen from others, he can see the potential for targeting the red product toward twenty-year-old males as the first big splash in the new market. He knows that he's looking at a spring timeframe based on the business case his team has built for the expansion.

So, he calls Mary, a marketing manager, or he walks down to her office and asks her to run the numbers for how the red product performed in the spring with twenty-year-old males.

At this point, you can see how the CEO dove pretty deep into the weeds because he's working on a business opportunity and

146

he has already begun to solve for it. How about that? He's in the Solution himself!

Here's what happens next. Few managers would challenge what they're asked to do, and Mary doesn't. So, she runs those numbers and produces a nice report for how the red product performed over the last three spring seasons with the twenty-year-old demographic.

It is a few days later before Mary is pulled into a meeting to report her findings. From the information the CEO gave her, she assumes the group is going to talk about how to build a launch campaign for the red product and to forecast revenues based on how this red product performed in other markets during the same season.

What Mary doesn't realize is that the CEO has dealt with several other issues since he made that request. The CEO may not remember what he was solving for at the time or he may have gotten additional input that moved him away from the red product or the twenty-year-old demographic.

So, when Mary shows up focused on solving for the red product and selling to twenty-year-old males, she's going to get blindsided by questions like this:

"How did the other three products perform with the same audience in the same timeframe?"

"Who was our strongest audience for the red product in the spring? Do the products seem to be seasonal?"

"Which product drove the highest brand awareness three months after launch? Was this consistent across all of our markets?"

As you can see, the CEO is back up at ten thousand feet and is now articulating what he was actually solving for all along. He wants to consider how all of his products would perform in terms of revenue and brand recognition. But, because he had a hypothesis of what the answer might be, he asked for a level of detail that narrowed Mary's focus.

Here's the real unfortunate part. Mary won't show up well because the questions will be out of context for her. She will struggle with responses, and her answers will sound tentative. She knows this isn't the place to blurt out, "That isn't what you asked for two days ago," but that's how she's feeling.

And, when she leaves the room, the CEO will lean over to her manager and say, "You know, Mary really struggles with strategic conversations. She always seems to miss the mark and the point of our discussions. I'm not sure you should keep bringing her to these strategy meetings."

Now we're back to the perspective of the middleman. Mary's boss thinks his judgment is in question, and Mary's moments of visibility have become a liability.

We've come full circle from where our conversation started at the beginning of the book. This time, the executive is causing the disconnect that exists. Mary could have done a great job of framing the Situation, the Solution and the Impact, but she had the wrong context to get started.

This is a common blind spot for executives. They forget who knows what, and they don't always give the context needed to help managers show up well. You have to learn to ask for it.

So, let's rewind to the point when the CEO walks down to Mary's office. Imagine if Mary had said, "I'll be happy to develop an analysis of how the red product performed with twenty-year-old males in the spring. Tell me what you're trying to solve for."

This would have triggered the CEO to share a little more context and could easily have gotten the conversation up a level or two. If the CEO had said in response, "I'm thinking about which products we should lead with in our new initiative and some data suggests it's the red product targeted to the twenty-year-old male." A manager who knows the space would probably have said, "That makes sense. Maybe I should compare all of the products to confirm that hunch."

We've talked a lot about how managers get stuck in the weeds. CEOs may go there, but they don't get stuck. They easily pop back up to ten thousand feet when prompted. Remember it's the altitude they operate from most of the time. "What are you trying to solve for?" has become a magic phrase to trigger context with leaders.

In our scenario, Mary's point of vulnerability could easily have been a moment of great recognition if only she had had the right assignment from the beginning.

Yet, managers are timid about asking for clarity. They just do what they're asked to do over and over again. Through the years, I've seen hundreds of presentations and reports that were based on an assignment without context. These scenarios never end well for the managers.

I've seen it enough to recognize that this disconnect exists, but managers don't lead these conversations every day so they often experience the heat before they have a chance to get comfortable sitting around the fire.

Another version of the same problem occurs in meetings when managers are asked questions they can't answer. Consider this question that Mary might be asked in our scenario. "Mary, we are currently looking at these trends for the Midwest market. Do you think the trends would show the same thing if we were launching in California first?"

Mary doesn't have the data to answer that question. So, she says I'm not sure and she leaves the meeting focused on getting that answer for the senior leaders. In Mary's case, it might take a day, but in many cases, it can take weeks to get data points and market intelligence. And, there was no confirmation that the executives actually wanted the data.

My experience is that some of the time, they actually don't want the data. They simply raise the question because they're thinking ahead or outside the box. They don't actually know what Mary knows and what she doesn't.

If Mary had said to the CEO, "That's an interesting question. I don't know the answer. Would you like me to run a market analysis on California?" There's a good chance he might have said, "No, we're not ready to focus on that market. I was just curious about it."

Senior leaders are curious, and it's what makes them good at what they do. They consider things outside the lines and way ahead of the plan. Unintentionally, they can cause departments to spin their wheels simply because someone didn't ask for more context.

It may seem simple in the scenario, but it isn't quite so simple when you're in the middle of it. Managers don't know what they don't know, and executives forget who's been in different conversations. It's just a gap in perspectives.

We've come full circle in our discussion of perspectives. I started the book talking about the perspective that many managers were missing, and now we're close to the end focused on the perspective that executives miss. It happens both ways, but in either case, it's the manager who needs to know how to rectify it. Here are two tools that will help you do that.

First, adjust the altitude. The conversation can be too broad like the California market or too narrow like the red product sold to twenty-year-old males in the spring. We use the visual of a funnel again to help managers understand that they want to get any question to the right altitude. We called it your sweet spot as noted in the diagram. The idea is to pull the topic up or down to fit within the knowledge that you have.

Meeting: Midwest Market Launch
Questions:

"Do you think the trends would show the same thing
if we were launching in California first?"

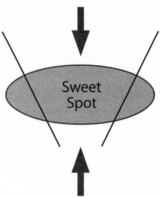

"What are the numbers for how the red product
performed in the spring with twenty-year-old males?"

In the scenario, Mary's sweet spot is somewhere in between the two extremes. When she got the question in the weeds, she needed to pull the conversation up by saying, "What are you solving for? Do you want to know how all the products performed in the spring with three target audiences?"

When she got the question out of scope or at too high an altitude, she needed to pull it down by saying, "Our analysis was focused only on trends in the Midwest, so I don't have data for you on California. Is that something you want to consider at this point?"

Both examples focus on getting the question to the right altitude. We use this technique to teach people how to answer questions, and it works very effectively with a senior audience.

The second tool is to ask for context. I mentioned that executives are curious by nature, and they don't mind curiosity returned. In fact, I think some executives use it as a measure of leadership potential. Many have said through the years that they're more intrigued by what managers ask than by what managers give as answers. Your questions give them insight into how you think. More importantly, their responses will give insight into what they think.

Not every situation requires clarification, and you won't always have access to an executive to get it. But, you can use the framework as a constant tool to be thinking about the elements of a discussion that all parties need. It's the Situation that helps everyone understand what we're solving and why we want to solve it. Once that's in place, it's much easier to gain alignment around how things should be solved.

In fact, in many organizations I notice that senior leaders align quickly with managers who can regulate the altitude and clarify context. It's common to see an executive become dependent on a manager who knows how to ask the questions or reframe the request to get to what the executive needs.

Chapter 7 talked about the executives need for context, and managers need it as well. Be cautious of taking on an assignment without context because often you will find that what executives initially ask for isn't always what they want.

20

The Final Word

"I expected you to help me organize my thoughts; instead, you gave me the confidence to drive an outcome. It's the most important thing I've learned in my career to date."

When we coach people to deliver effective presentations, we call the end of the presentation "the final word." And, we have arrived at that point on the topic of executive conversations. So, here are my final thoughts.

My goal in writing this book was twofold. By sharing my experiences and stories from working with hundreds of managers and executives, I wanted to give managers a better understanding of why executive conversations can be difficult. By understanding that there will always be different perspectives, it makes it a little easier to pull them closer together.

I also wanted to share the tools that we've used to help managers turn visibility moments into career opportunities. It isn't a magical formula as much as it is a proven approach. Reading this book won't make it easier overnight. It takes practice to put the tools in place and to think about these conversations from both perspectives.

But it works. After every workshop, we get notes like the quote underneath the chapter title that confirm the impact of the concepts I've shared with you. Some managers write to share the success of a high-level conversation. Others write to share job promotions, approval of major initiatives or buy-in to a different approach. We hear about projects moving faster, groups reaching consensus, and budgets gaining approval.

For every manager who has written to share a success after our workshop, there is also the manager who laments that someone should have shared this kind of information sooner. That gets to the real value of this book. I hope that our insights and our tools have reached you at the right time in your career to help you turn a high-level conversation into a real opportunity.

I opened with the phrase: be careful what you ask for. But, with the tools in hand, you will be ready for those high visibility moments. Executive conversations carry risks, but they also carry rewards. I hope you'll let us know what you accomplish.

Appendix

Survey Results

Survey administered by Fitzgerald+CO
April 16 - May 17, 2013

Importance of Executive-Level Meetings

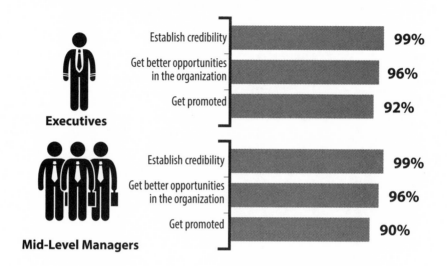

Executives

- Establish credibility — **99%**
- Get better opportunities in the organization — **96%**
- Get promoted — **92%**

Mid-Level Managers

- Establish credibility — **99%**
- Get better opportunities in the organization — **96%**
- Get promoted — **90%**

Impressions of Mid-Level Managers

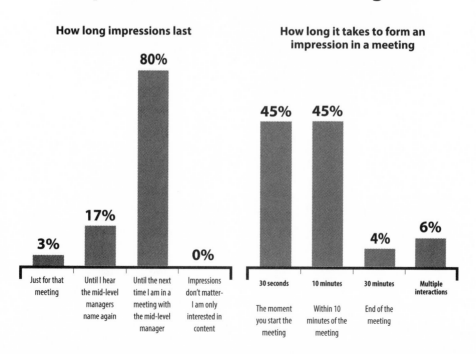

How long impressions last

3%	**17%**	**80%**	**0%**
Just for that meeting	Until I hear the mid-level managers name again	Until the next time I am in a meeting with the mid-level manager	Impressions don't matter- I am only interested in content

How long it takes to form an impression in a meeting

45%	**45%**	**4%**	**6%**
30 seconds	10 minutes	30 minutes	**Multiple interactions**
The moment you start the meeting	Within 10 minutes of the meeting	End of the meeting	

Outcomes of
Executive-Level Meetings

Executives

Mid-Level Managers

29% of these meetings are
perceived to be run poorly

39% of these meetings do not
achieve intended results

Are Executive Meetings More
Challenging than Other Meetings?

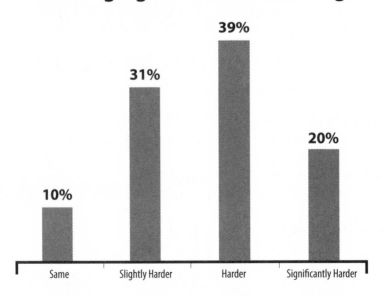

10%	31%	39%	20%
Same	Slightly Harder	Harder	Significantly Harder

Challenging Aspects of Executive-Level Meetings

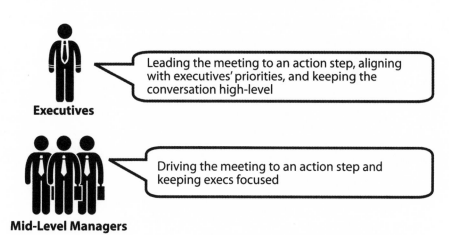

Executives

Leading the meeting to an action step, aligning with executives' priorities, and keeping the conversation high-level

Mid-Level Managers

Driving the meeting to an action step and keeping execs focused

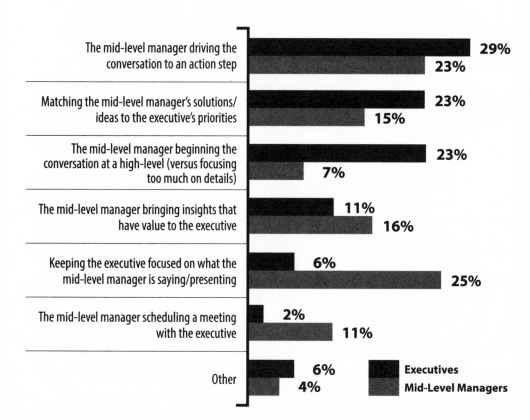

The mid-level manager driving the conversation to an action step — **29%** / **23%**

Matching the mid-level manager's solutions/ideas to the executive's priorities — **23%** / **15%**

The mid-level manager beginning the conversation at a high-level (versus focusing too much on details) — **23%** / **7%**

The mid-level manager bringing insights that have value to the executive — **11%** / **16%**

Keeping the executive focused on what the mid-level manager is saying/presenting — **6%** / **25%**

The mid-level manager scheduling a meeting with the executive — **2%** / **11%**

Other — **6%** / **4%**

Executives
Mid-Level Managers

What Makes Executive Meetings Unsuccessful for Executives?

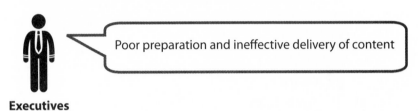

Poor preparation and ineffective delivery of content

Executives

You ask things they are unprepared to answer	**57%**
The mid-level manager presents too much detail—not high-level enough	**56%**
The mid-level manager isn't able to make his/her point effectively	**55%**
You don't get a clear takeaway from the mid-level manager	**55%**
You sidetrack the meeting to get the information you need	**51%**
The mid-level manager doesn't get through planned material	**50%**
The mid-level manager loses your attention	**48%**
The mid-level manager loses control of the meeting	**48%**
The mid-level manager loses his/her focus	**44%**
You were not clear about what he/she is presenting	**43%**
The mid-level manager gets frazzled/nervous	**41%**
The meeting gets cut short	**41%**
You ask things that are not related to the meeting topic	**40%**

What Makes Executive Meetings Unsuccessful for Mid-Level Managers?

Feeling rushed by the executive

Mid-Level Managers

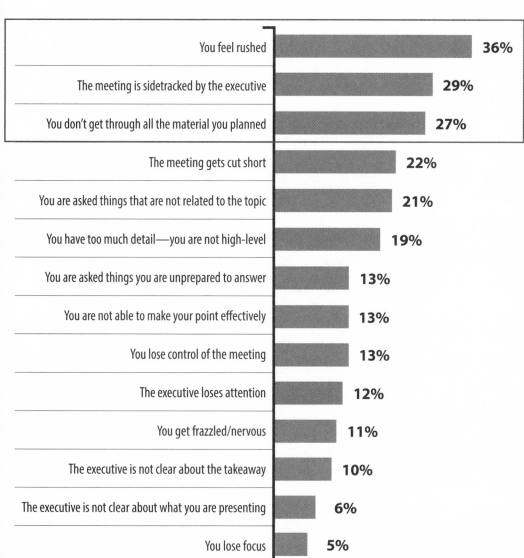

Well-Run Executive Meetings Include:

Executives

Relevant and timely topics

Topic relevant and timely	**100%**
Clear understanding of what manager needs from executive	**98%**
Clear recommendation or solution tied to topic	**98%**
Topic aligned with business need	**96%**
Clear data points	**93%**
Possible outcomes or results indicated	**91%**
Good external perspective provided	**63%**
Industry comparisons and best practices	**63%**

Ways to Capture
an Executive's Attention

Executives

The ideal length of an executive meeting is 30 minutes

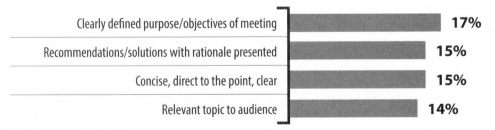

Clearly defined purpose/objectives of meeting	**17%**
Recommendations/solutions with rationale presented	**15%**
Concise, direct to the point, clear	**15%**
Relevant topic to audience	**14%**

Preparation Strategies

Executives

Mid-Level Managers

Executives emphasize gaining an internal perspective on the issue

Both executives and mid-level managers consider discussing the agenda with execs as most important when preparing for the meeting

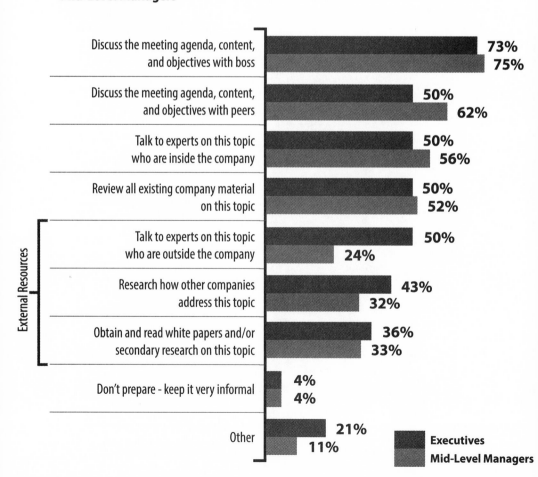

	Executives	Mid-Level Managers
Discuss the meeting agenda, content, and objectives with boss	73%	75%
Discuss the meeting agenda, content, and objectives with peers	50%	62%
Talk to experts on this topic who are inside the company	50%	56%
Review all existing company material on this topic	50%	52%
Talk to experts on this topic who are outside the company	50%	24%
Research how other companies address this topic	43%	32%
Obtain and read white papers and/or secondary research on this topic	36%	33%
Don't prepare - keep it very informal	4%	4%
Other	21%	11%

External Resources

Structuring the Meeting – Key Topics

While both executives and managers find all elements of a meeting useful, executives are most interested in preparation and the context of the Situation. Managers tend to invest their time in the details of the Solution and Next Steps.

Executives

Mid-Level Managers

Pre-Meeting
Preparation

- Clear objective with key stakeholders
- Know audience & their preferred styles
- Send agenda & materials ahead of time
- Anticipate questions

Meeting
Situation

- State purpose of meeting
- State expectation & takeaway
- Background
- Research
- Issue / challenge

Solution

- Status update
- Data points
- Recommendations & rationale
  - » Options
  - » Timeline

**Impact /
Next Steps**

- Summary
- The ask
- Next steps / action items
  - » Follow-up expectations
  - » Q&A / feedback

Resources

What Managers Are Saying About Our Workshop

"The framework really helped me move past just knowing the conversation should be different, to knowing how to reframe it."

"You broadened my thinking about perspectives. By taking time to think through the executive perspective, I am more confident and more aligned in every meeting."

"I absolutely use the framework to be prepared for executive meetings! I think through my purpose, decision, and outcome."

"The workshop helped me to identify ways to gain and retain an executive's attention, and now I feel that I do that effectively."

"Last month you all helped me prepare for my executive conversation regarding a new opportunity. Well, I'm very happy to share that I received word back today, and they extended me an offer to join the team!"

"I still think about the concept of earning my right to be in front of the executive and the importance of the first two minutes."

"It has been a game changer to learn how to frame up what I'm asking for and why it is important to the organization."

"The executive meeting I had after the class was a success. I was able to present my points, gain their support for my recommendation, and they all agreed and accepted the recommendation as the decision going forward. I will look for other courses your team provides!"

"This was by far the best program I have participated in, and I have a current opportunity to apply what I have learned."

"Messaging has really helped me build my credibility, and the flow of the meeting goes very well when I state the end at the beginning."

"I found the session extremely useful and plan on incorporating many of the concepts into my approach moving forward. I plan on recommending this class to my peers as well."

Template:
Executive Conversation

MESSAGE

The Message is one sentence; it's the bottom line. A message sets up what you're asking the executive to consider.

If we *(do this – the ask of the business)*, we will *(get this – the business outcome or impact)*.

OVERVIEW OF FRAMEWORK

The Overview highlights the flow of the conversation.

SITUATION

The Situation provides context for the topic starting with an external perspective and drilling down to the opportunity or problem to be solved.

EXTERNAL PERSPECTIVE

INTERNAL PERSPECTIVE

SPECIFIC PROGRAM OR INITIATIVES

WHAT I'M SOLVING FOR

SOLUTION

The Solution describes how the opportunity will be explored or how the issue will be resolved.

IMPACT / NEXT STEPS

The Impact proves the business outcome and benefit with measurable results. It also provides a next step to move the recommendation forward.

Example:
Executive Conversation Scenario

SCENARIO

You are a marketing manager for a consumer products company that launched a mobile app last year. You've had a great response to the app (over 30,000 people have already downloaded it), but to date, those downloads haven't turned into a significant lift in your sales. Your team has put time and effort into analyzing why the leads don't create sales, and you've learned from industry studies that it takes four visits to an app to generate a sale. You've explored best practices to keep an app active, and gaming seems to be the most innovative concept that companies are using to generate repeat interest. You'd like to get the EVP of sales and marketing interested in this, and you're meeting with him to ask for initial funding to develop a game concept that could be launched in six months.

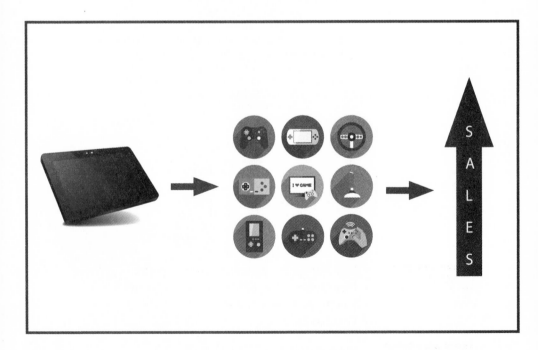

Example:
Executive Conversation

MESSAGE

If we enhance the consumer's experience with a gaming concept, we should triple visits to our mobile app and increase product sales in six months.

OVERVIEW OF FRAMEWORK

Today, I want to talk about:
- Best practices with apps and how to get results (Situation)
- A gaming solution that will help us get repeat visits (Solution)
- And, the results we could see in just six months (Impact)

SITUATION

EXTERNAL PERSPECTIVE
Define the size/growth of the smartphone marketplace.
Most apps on smartphones: generate visits but not sales.
Best practices say it takes four visits to get the user's attention.
Companies who get four visits have a gaming concept.

INTERNAL PERSPECTIVE
Our app has created awareness with the audiences we want.
Initial downloads exceeded expectations.
Our app is recognized for its look and ease of use.
We expanded our profile with the targeted demographic.

SPECIFIC PROGRAM OR INITIATIVES
Our experience: high downloads, low return visits.
Drop-off is significant after two visits.
We need a reason for customers to keep coming back.

WHAT I'M SOLVING FOR
Can we get users to return four or more times?
Gaming is the best practice.
Here's how I'd like to do it.

SOLUTION

- How games are developed and integrated
- Investment in a pilot to evaluate three options
- Funding and resource team
- Possible vendors

IMPACT / NEXT STEPS

- Prove product sales in six months
- Next Step: Buy-in from CTO and request for resources

Example:
Executive Overview (Pre-Read)

MEETING TOPIC

Discuss ways to generate more sales from our app.

MY ASK

Approve initial investment to pilot a gaming concept.

KEY TAKEAWAY

If we enhance the consumer's experience with a gaming concept, we should triple visits to our mobile app and increase product sales in six months.

SITUATION

We have had great response to the app we released last year. Over 30,000 people have downloaded the app, and we've been ranked as one of the top 20 sites in our industry. But, like many other companies, we aren't generating sales from initial interest. We evaluated best practices and learned that the difference between apps that generate sales and those that just generate interest is linked to the number of visits to the app. Research shows that it takes four visits to generate a sale. We have to triple visits to get sales, and we believe the addition of a gaming concept will help us do that.

SOLUTION

With initial funding of $50,000, we can test three of the most common gaming formats with a pilot group. Games are generally developed and tested with a pilot group of 200. The pilot requires both real time observation of how the games are played and then survey results from the players. We would run these pilots in four key markets to test for interests in different regions. Once we identify the right gaming format for our targeted audience, most vendors can develop the app in four months. Successful games require an enhancement or update every three months, so we will need resources to manage and support the app beyond what we're doing today.

IMPACT

We used several studies to measure the success of apps. Data points show not only an initial sale, but also great trends around recurring sales because of continued interest in returning to the site. I'll share specific data to support our estimate for sales impact within six months.

NEXT STEPS

As a result of our discussion, I hope to gain your buy-in for a gaming pilot and your help in scheduling a conversation with our CTO to explain the impact on our current hosting arrangement and potential IT resources needed to help us develop a product roadmap.

Example:
Executive Overview (Visual)

Meeting: **Wednesday, August 28th, 2:00. p.m – 2:30 p.m.**

| TOPIC | Generating sales from our app |

| ASK | Initial investment to pilot a gaming concept |

| MESSAGE | If we enhance the consumer's experience with a gaming concept, we should triple visits to our mobile app and increase product sales in six months. |

Flow of Discussion:

| SITUATION | Best Practices with Apps
• Gaming generates 3x the interest of other tools |

| SOLUTION | Pilot Three Gaming Concepts
• Target four markets for quick input and action |

| IMPACT | Gaming Can Impact Sales
• Projected results from launch |

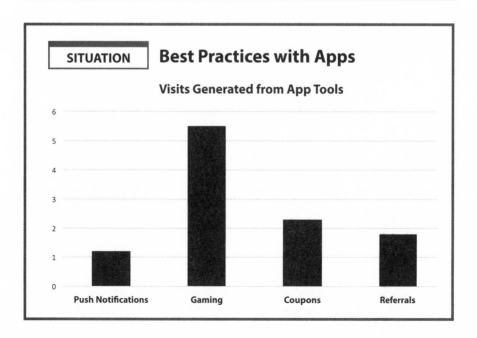

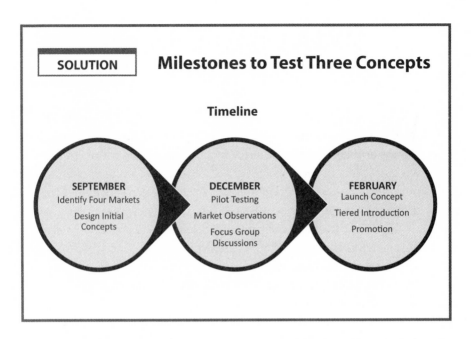

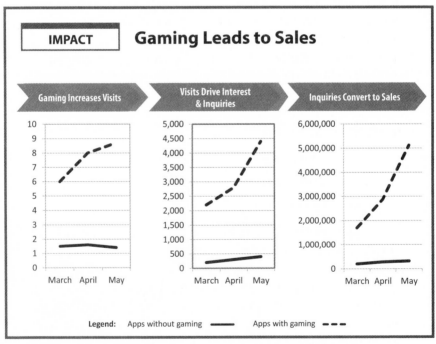

SW&A Content Planner

We created our online tool, the SW&A Content Planner, to support the methodology taught in our Effective Presentations and Leading Executive Conversations workshops. While we use it in our workshops, it is also a stand-alone tool that provides an easy and effective way to create messaging and to drive a clear storyline.

The Executive Conversations planner follows the process described in this book. You will be asked to create a compelling message, to develop a three-step framework - that includes Situation, Solution, and Impact/Next Steps - and to frame the Situation according to the funnel.

Our planner helps you map out a storyline for a conversation or a presentation. The content entered populates to the Planner Results page, which is a complete outline of the conversation. This is also where you can add examples and visual concepts. Finally, you can export the outline to a Word document, which makes it easy to edit and seek buy-in from others.

Why do you need a storyline? You want to make sure you have addressed the three most common things an executive or any audience listens for:

- What's your point?

- How are we going to get there?

- Prove the benefit

The planner helps you learn the discipline of developing a storyline, which is critical to the success of any conversation or presentation.

To access the planner, go to www.planapresentation.com. Create an account with a customized username and password. Then, log in to the tool and decide what level of access you would like. Either level gives you access to both the Effective Presentations and Executive Conversations planners.

Let us help you improve the impact of your spoken communications. Register to use the planner today!